shaken
not
STIRRED

THE BOTTLE, THE BIBLE,
AND THE BELIEVER

DAN FISHER

TATE PUBLISHING, LLC

Published in the United States of America
by Tate Publishing, LLC
127 East Trade Center Terrace
Mustang, OK 73064
(888) 361-9473

ISBN: 1-9332902-5-0

DEDICATION

I dedicate this book to the three people that mean the most to me: my wife, Pam, and my two children, Jacob and Rebekah. If God uses this book to any great degree, it is because of their influence and encouragement.

Pam, you are truly the love of my life. Other than salvation, of all the gifts God has given me in this life, I cherish you the most. Your unwavering, sacrificial love and support continue to be a major force in molding me into the man God wants me to be. Your love and devotion to Jesus inspire me. Your knowledge of and commitment to God's Word exhort me. I shudder to think of where I would be without you. I love you and consider it an honor that you would share your life with me.

Jacob, every father wants his son to be a better man than he is—you are. Quite possibly, my greatest work for God in this life will be the privilege of being your dad. Of all my responsibilities, I consider this one to be most important. Your love for the Lord and quiet, yet confident spirit are contagious. I am confident that your own service to the Lord and His kingdom will far eclipse my own. I look forward to watching God's plan unfold in your life. I love you and am proud of you, my son.

Rebekah, a father's daughter is normally the "apple of his eye" and you certainly are for me. Early in life, I feared having a daughter who would be like me. You have proved how wrong my fears were. Although you are very much like me, God took what little good He found in me, mixed it with your mother and His grace and made the masterpiece we call Rebekah. You are God's special gift sent to soften my heart. Your fun personality and sense of humor always bring light into the room. Your keen sense of right and wrong and your desire to serve others are a reflection of Christ in you. You are becoming a woman of grace whom, I am confident, God will use in mighty ways. Always remember, your dad loves you.

$\mathscr{A}$CKNOWLEDGEMENTS

All authors owe many people a great deal of gratitude. I am no different. Although I could mention many others, I would like to express my special thanks to the following:

Mom: You taught me from my earliest years about Jesus and lived a sacrificial life for me. You are a part of, and have an investment in, everything I do for God. I love you.

Alan, Stacy, & Luke Baker: Your friendship and support have helped carry me through some difficult times. Stacy, this book would not have happened without you. Alan, you saved my bacon on the house–how can I ever repay you? All I can say is: you're King of the World! Luke, you encourage me. Remember me when you come into your kingdom.

Joel & Valerie Engle: Your friendship and encouragement over the years have been invaluable. It's a joy to see God using you to transform countless lives. One of those lives is my own. Thanks for staying true to the Word.

Linda Costilow: You're the best! You keep me between the ditches. I wouldn't get a thing done without you. You make me look better than I really am–thank you.

Scott & Sue Kinney: From the earliest days, you have believed in me. Thanks for being there through the good times and the bad. Scott, thanks for standing up for me when few did; you are indeed a true friend.

Bill Kramer: Thanks for being willing to recommend my book. I appreciate your faith in me and this project.

Trinity congregation, staff, & elders: Thank you for your patience and trust. You have tolerated my stumbling attempts at leadership and have allowed me to learn what it truly means to attempt to build a prevailing church. I consider it an honor to labor together with you as we try to make a real difference for Christ.

Congregation of Immanuel Baptist, Poteau, OK: Thank you for taking the gamble on a young, unproven, wet-behind-the-ears preacher. I hope your faith and investment in me was not wasted. Regardless of where the Lord may lead, you'll always be in my heart.

TABLE OF CONTENTS

Foreword

There are few people I have ever known who really know the Bible like Dan Fisher. I have seen Dan's life as a pastor under the most difficult of situations. There is no one I respect more. Dan's ministry is marked by a deep, consistent love for God's Word. So when he told me he was writing a book I said, "It's about time!"

It is possible for one to understand philosophy, science, or even theology but miss the wondrous and heart-melting truths of God's Word. For the Christian, however, the Bible is the only standard by which we measure truth. Secular humanism and pop culture have so greatly influenced modern Christian thinking that we have become lost in our understanding of social issues and how to deal with them in the reality of our daily lives. Christians are people of the "Book" and we must get back to the "Book" to find our answers to life's tough questions.

The subject of alcohol is no different. So many lives have been forever ruined by the abuse of it. There are many different viewpoints on how we, as Christians, are to respond to alcohol. Can we drink a small glass of wine privately or should we abstain completely? Where is the balance between legalism and grace? What does church history say about drinking? Didn't Jesus turn water into wine? These are all legitimate questions that need to be answered for every Christian. Dan takes us to the "Book" to find out what God says about this most controversial subject.

To be honest, I have floated back and forth over this issue in my own mind and ministry. Am I being a legalist by completely abstaining from alcohol, or would it be harmless to have one innocent glass of wine on some random, private occasion? Praise God for Dan Fisher and this book! Dan takes a totally honest look historically, philosophically, and most importantly, he takes a solid biblical look at the Christian's response to alcohol. God has used this study to lead me to a clear decision on how I will respond to drinking for the rest of my life. The great thing about it is that I don't feel guilty of legalism or of abusing the grace of God because I have clearly seen what the Scriptures have to say about it. Jesus was right: "The truth shall make you free." You will be blessed and seriously challenged by reading this book.

Blessings to you in Christ,
Joel Engle
Worship Leader and Christian recording artist,
Doxology Records

Chapter 1

S HAKEN, NOT STIRRED

The evening had been slow. John Parker's assignment for the night was a particularly boring one. He sat there trying to pass the time but every minute seemed like an hour. As he was prone to do, he began to develop a terrible thirst for a drink. He and a couple of his friends, Charles and Francis, discussed taking a quick trip to a nearby saloon. John thought, *Surely I could go with them, after all, nothing has happened all night—I won't be missed for a few minutes.* He looked around making certain that nothing needed his immediate attention, checked his watch, and then abandoned his post to accompany his buddies to Taltavul's Star Saloon next door.

When they arrived at Taltavul's, they found the saloon dimly lit with a cloud of cigar smoke hanging in the stale air. As Parker and his friends made a beeline to the bar for a drink, another man (also named John) who had become quite famous over the past few years, sat at his table in deep thought. He too, badly needed a drink, but for a different reason—he was trying to drum up some courage. Staring into space, totally oblivious to the world around him, the man seemed lost in deep thought as if the future of the world hinged on his next move.

Busy with drinking and meaningless conversation, Parker and his friends lost track of time, ignoring the fact that they should report back for duty. They never noticed when the man at the table left the saloon. Suddenly, they were shaken into reality by excited shouts. As the room quieted, everyone learned the horrible truth—the President had been shot!

Although some of this narrative is speculative, the two Johns in this story are real—they were John Parker and John Wilkes Booth. John Parker was the Washington police officer who had been given the responsibility of guarding President Abraham Lincoln on the night of April 14, 1865 as the President and Mrs. Lincoln attended the play, *Our American Cousin,* at Ford's Theater. The other John—John Wilkes Booth—as everyone knows, is the man who assassinated President Lincoln. The two other men, Charles and Francis, were Charles Forbes, the President's footman, and Francis P. Burke, the President's coachman.

John Parker's part in the story of President Lincoln's assassination is shrouded in mystery. His exact role in the assassination plot, if any, was never determined. Although tried for dereliction of duty, Parker was never convicted of any crime and remained on the Washington police force until he was dismissed for sleeping on duty in 1868. Even though his record as a policeman is somewhat dubious, what *is* known is that Parker had been a policeman since the founding of the Washington D.C. Metropolitan Police Force in 1861 and that he did have a strong propensity for alcohol. Despite the fact that the exact activities of John Parker on the night of April 14, 1865 will probably never be known, this fact is certain: he left his post as guard of the door to the Presidential box at Ford's Theater to have a drink at the saloon next door with Forbes and Burke. What is also known is that, ironically, Booth visited the same saloon for a drink of "liquid courage" (quite possibly at the same time Parker was also there) just before he made his way next door to shoot the President.

Imagine how history would have been vastly different if, when Booth reached the door to the Presidential box, he had found a sober John Parker on duty. But alas, it was not to be. Alcohol's call was stronger in John Parker than the call of duty, so the President and the whole nation suffered the consequences. What a price to pay for a drink.

I wonder what excuse John Parker gave for drinking that night—what excuse could he have given? What have been the excuses of the millions who have consumed alcohol through the centuries? What excuses do people give today? There has to be a reason why people are willing to gamble with alcohol's harmful effects. Does it make their lives better? Do they really like the taste of it that much? Is it just a habit? Is it an addiction? Is it peer pressure? Maybe their reasoning is something like this:

- It's Friday night after the game and his high school buddies are urging him to take his first drink. "Come on," they say, "you don't know what you're missing. Go ahead, take a drink; we won't tell anyone—especially your parents." What should he do? He really wants to fit in with the gang. How much damage could just one drink do?
- "Are you coming over to the frat house tonight? It'll be the best party ever with plenty of booze and girls. Everybody's gonna be there. See you at six." He's finally out of high school and is beginning to experience real freedom for the very first time in his life. Should he go? After all, isn't partying supposed to be a big part of the college experience anyway?
- With high hopes and bright futures, two newlyweds with arms intertwined, clink champagne glasses together as they toast one another at the reception. Family and friends raise their glasses toward the couple joining the toast, celebrating the moment together. What's the problem with that? After all, it's a wedding.
- A few couples celebrating a night out on the town, order wine with their meal. Surely nothing could be wrong with that. For Pete's sake, they're not going to get drunk.
- The crowd roars as the running back crosses the goal line. The beer man is only a few rows away, so what's the harm in having a cup? Almost everyone else is.
- He pops open a beer to quench his powerful thirst as he sits down in his patio lounge chair. Who doesn't drink a cold one after getting all hot and sweaty from mowing the lawn? Give me a break!
- All the guys are having a few beers as they sit around the campfire. He's on a hunting trip and that's just what everybody does

in the great outdoors. He has worked hard all year and he's earned it. Can he really say he's been in deer camp if he hasn't had a few beers?

- He's on a business trip. It's been a difficult, but successful one. The stewardess asks if he would like a drink. He thinks, "I'm miles from home, no one here knows me, so what could possibly be wrong with it?" Surely it isn't going to hurt anyone if he uses a drink to help him relax a little, is it?

- His boss reminds him on the way to the restaurant that these clients are important to the company's future. They always want to mix business with pleasure, so the firm always pays for a night out on the town. His boss tells him that it won't hurt anybody if he has a few drinks. He reminds him that it is the only polite thing to do and besides, it might help seal the deal. How can he refuse such logic?

- A young father wants to celebrate the birth of his first child. His buddies suggest that they go to a nearby bar for drinks. What should he do? Isn't a new father supposed to spring for a few drinks after his child is born?

Any of this sound familiar? Many often find themselves in such situations. For years they've justified their drinking with similar arguments. But what should a believer do when faced with such dilemmas? Does the Bible really say?

As a pastor for more than twenty-two years, I have repeatedly been asked this question. People want to know what the Bible says about the believer and alcohol. Since there is tremendous interest and debate over this issue, my desire is to offer a fair, realistic, and biblical discussion. Realizing that equally sincere believers are on both sides of this debate, I do not desire to appear legalistic or judgmental. At the same time, I believe this issue is so critical to the church, it demands an honest investigation of the facts.

One hundred and thirty-three years ago, a pastor by the name of William Patton faced this same issue. He found, as I do today, that there was a tendency, worse yet, *a desire* among Christians to use alcohol. In the introduction of his historic book, *Bible Wines or Laws of Fermentation and Wines of the Ancients,* he wrote:

> "I soon found that the concession so generally made even by ministers, that the Bible sanctions the use of intoxicating drinks, was the most impregnable citadel into which all drinkers, all apologists for drinking, and all venders of the article, fled. This compelled me, thus early, to study the Bible patiently and carefully, to know for myself its exact teachings . . . Each age of the Church has, as it were, turned over a new leaf in the Bible, and found a response to its own wants. We have a leaf to turn—a leaf not the less new because it is so simple."[1]

This is exactly why I feel so compelled to write this book. Once again, the Church needs to "turn a leaf" and reexamine the Bible's teachings on alcohol, clarifying what the believer's attitude toward it should be. In the book of Hosea we read:

> "my people are destroyed from lack of knowledge. Because you have rejected knowledge, I also reject you as my priests; because you have ignored the law of your God, I also will ignore your children." Hosea 4:6, NIV

"Shaken, not stirred." Ian Fleming's legendary secret agent, James Bond, was famous for using these words when ordering his martinis. His taste in liquor has, in a strangely symbolic way, become the response of thousands in the church.

This phrase is all too often representative of the blasé attitude many believers have about alcohol today. When confronted with what the Scriptures say about drinking, they sometimes appear "shaken," but not "stirred"—certainly not stirred enough to consider the possibility that drinking might be wrong. I am convinced that church leaders are greatly to blame for this general attitude having done a poor job of communicating the biblical truths about alcohol over the years. When they have addressed the subject, often their message, rather than being informational and inspirational, has been judgmental leaving the hearers so "turned off" that the Bible's position on alcohol has remained unknown to numerous generations of the church. It is my hope that this book will so stir believers that they will be forced to seriously consider whether or not their position on alcohol is biblical.

Since I'm relatively certain that studying alcohol-related statistical data is not on most people's Saturday to-do list and that most probably don't consider a fact book about alcohol as recreational reading, I've attempted to make learning the facts easier. I've gathered many pertinent and compelling data from some of the most recent and authoritative studies available. By taking an honest look at these facts, I believe we can give informed answers to such questions as:

- Why do people drink?
- Do drinkers seriously consider the consequences of drinking?
- How much damage does alcohol really do?
- Did those in Bible times regularly drink intoxicating wines?
- How does our drinking affect others?
- Should a believer use alcohol?

I realize that what I say in this book will thrill some while infuriating others. Therefore, I encourage you, the reader, to study this entire presentation before making up your mind concerning its message. While reading this book, I encourage you to ask yourself, "Does a Christian have a legitimate need to drink alcohol? What good ever comes from drinking?"

I'm sure that some may be saying, "Of course he's against drinking, after all, he's a Baptist preacher—what else would you expect him to believe?" It's true that Baptists have traditionally been known as those who: "Don't drink, dance, smoke, or chew and don't date the girls who do!" And admittedly some among the Baptist ranks have been overly legalistic about such things over the years; however, does this completely invalidate the stand that the more reasonably-minded Baptists have traditionally taken against alcohol? (To be fair, Baptists have not been the only ones who have stood against drinking over the years—many others have also preached against the destructive power of alcohol). Charlie, a good friend of mine, has a lighthearted way of looking at it. He jokingly says, "People just don't get it—alcohol isn't the problem. The reason Baptists are against alcohol is because when people drink, they dance, and everyone knows that dancing is the real sin!"

Although we can have a good laugh at that type of thinking, the truth is, we really do need to know what we believe about alcohol and why. Knowing the reasons for our beliefs is so important that we can't resort to catchy clichés, to denomination/tradition-based creeds, or to "grandma always said" opinions. Instead, we must seriously examine God's Word and discover what it actually says. Once we do this, it really won't matter what others think or say, because we will have an unshakeable set of convictions built on the solid bedrock of Scripture rather than the shifting sands of popular opinion.

It is my prayer that God will use this work to help believers do just that—discover what the Bible teaches about alcohol and build a strong defense against arguments that would say otherwise. It is also my hope that this book can serve both as a defense to those who are tempted by alcohol's siren song and as a means of deliverance for those already mesmerized by its spell. To this end, I dedicate this work.

Chapter 2

Ⓢ TORIES THE COMMERCIALS DON'T TELL

The call came unexpectedly—the call a pastor hopes he'll never receive. The voice on the other end said that Natalie, the daughter of a couple in our church, had been killed by a drunk driver. The caller proceeded to give me the details of what had happened. Natalie and a group of her friends had gone to Padre Island for spring break along with an aunt of one of the girls who went along as their chaperone. While they were walking back to their hotel, a drunk driver lost control of his vehicle traveling at approximately 65 mph, drove over the curb, and hit Natalie sending her flying through the air. The impact broke her neck, killing her instantly. Her friends, who miraculously escaped injury, said that it happened so quickly; they were certain Natalie never even knew what hit her.

As I sat there holding the phone, I felt nauseated. I didn't know what to say. The whole tragedy was so senseless and so avoidable. What made Natalie's murder even more insidious was that the driver of the truck had gotten his alcohol from a temporary bar that specifically targeted students who spent their spring break in Padre. What a perfect recipe for disaster: spring break, students, and alcohol. At the close of spring break, the operators of the temporary bar would close it up and launder their profits through another corporation making it virtually impossible for authorities to hold them responsible for any damage they had caused.

It is just as impossible to describe the wide range of emotions Natalie's family experienced in the days immediately following her death—feelings of hurt, frustration, rage, and inexplicable grief. I struggled with what to say at the funeral. Put yourself in my shoes—what do you say at the funeral of a beautiful young lady like Natalie whose hopes and dreams have been erased by the careless, criminal act of a drunk? What do you say to her mother who will never get to help plan her wedding? What do you say to her father who will never get to walk her down the aisle?

With God's help, we got through it. In the years since, I have watched Natalie's parents continue to agonize over their loss. I've cried with them as they've relived her death again and again. They've watched with feelings of joy and pain as Natalie's friends have graduated, gone to college, and gotten married. I've listened as her parents have often talked of what might have been. I've watched them struggle through our legal system as they sought justice for Natalie—hoping their efforts would prevent other families from ever having to experience a similar tragedy. I have watched as those who operated the temporary bar, accessories to the crime, managed to circumvent the law, escaping any responsibility for Natalie's death. I've watched as Natalie's parents have run ads in the local newspaper each year reminding people not to forget her. Hoping to reduce the madness, they have spoken to community groups warning of the dangers of drinking and driving and they have reached out to people experiencing grief similar to their own. Their unshakeable faith in Jesus has enabled them to hold it all together and make something good out of something very bad. But no matter what good comes from her death, the fact remains—Natalie is gone.

One such tragedy would have been enough for me for an entire lifetime of ministry, but unfortunately it was not to be the last. Four years later, another call came.

This time it was Krystle, the daughter of another couple in our church, who had been killed in a car accident. I'll never forget the horror of that night. As my associate pastor and I drove to the hospital in Stillwater, OK, I kept asking myself, "What am I going to say to the family?" I wondered, "What words will help ease their pain and help them make some sense out of this nightmare?" *It's Natalie all over again,* I thought.

As we drove through the night toward the hospital, I tried to prepare for the difficult task that lay ahead. I remember wishing that I weren't a pastor and that I could drive the other way, but I knew that Krystle's family was experiencing one of the darkest moments of their lives and needed all of the support they could get.

As we pulled into the hospital parking lot and made our way to the emergency entrance, I sighed and took a deep breath, trying to collect my thoughts. I prayed, "God, please help us get through this."

The scene inside the hospital was heart-wrenching. Doctors and nurses were rushing from room to room attending to the injuries of Krystle's friends. Family and friends were seated everywhere—some praying, some crying, some clinging to one another, and some just staring into space unable to synthesize this surreal scene.

As we reached the door of the little room where Krystle's family had been taken, one of her friends was wheeled by us on a gurney. She needed surgery and was being transferred to a hospital in Oklahoma City. As I opened the door to the packed family room, I breathed the thick air of grief. Even though our hearts told us that Krystle was now in heaven, our emotions revealed our pain. The hurt in the room was so great that it seemed we could touch it. We did the only thing we could do—we cried and prayed.

In the hours that followed, we learned the details of the accident. Krystle and her three friends had been in her car returning from a Sunday School class fellowship when they had been hit head-on by a pick-up truck driven by a young man who was drunk. Confused by the brain-numbing effects of the alcohol, he was driving down the wrong side of the divided four-lane highway when he collided head-on with Krystle's car. The impact killed Krystle instantly and severely injured the other passengers in her car. As is often the case, the drunk driver escaped with minor injuries.

In the days, weeks, and months that followed, Krystle's family found the strength to go on. They made it through her funeral.

They endured the trial of Krystle's murderer as they, like Natalie's parents, sought justice—not revenge. They listened to the family and friends of the young man who killed Krystle as they testified to the court of his good life and high moral character. They listened as his attorneys painted the picture of a well-meaning, all-American boy who just made a bad mistake. They listened as the judge issued an incredibly mild sentence for such a heinous crime.

Since the trial, they've prayed that good will somehow come from their horrible ordeal. They have grieved but they have coped. They have spoken to numerous community groups trying to educate people about the dangers of drinking and driving. They have tried their best to adjust to life without their daughter.

Krystle's brothers have had to deal with the anger and frustration of having their sister literally stolen from them. The hole that was created in their hearts and lives has been impossible to fill. Having found the courage to go on, they now find themselves graduating from high school and going to college without their big sister's encouragement and advice. Krystle's parents have had to accept the fact that they will never get to be Grandpa and Grandma to her children, because thanks to alcohol, she won't have any. Alcohol takes away so much and then gives nothing but pain and emptiness in return.

These families and those of us who walked through their nightmare with them learned firsthand how alcohol can kill. But over the years, I've learned that alcohol can steal as well as kill. I've seen it steal morals, I've seen it steal reputations, and I've seen it steal promising futures. I've watched as fine young men and women started running with the wrong "friends". Before long, they were going to parties, drinking, and doing things they wouldn't have normally done. I've watched as their lives spiraled downward. I've prayed and counseled with their parents as they've desperately sought for ways to help their troubled sons and daughters. I've talked with these wayward children, warning them of the potential disasters looming on their horizons. But unfortunately for so many, alcohol's grip was so strong that it took a tragedy to jolt them into reality. Even then, some never got the message. I've watched students drop out of school, giving up promising careers. I've watched young girls become unwed mothers—facing for a whole lifetime, the consequences of their bad choices.

I've seen alcohol destroy marriages. I've seen it destroy businesses. I've seen it destroy friendships and I've seen it destroy careers. For example, the September 18, 2004 issue of *The Oklahoman* published an article chronicling the fall of Dusty Dvoracek, a star defensive tackle for the Oklahoma Sooners football team.[2] The article reported that because of his repeated infractions involving alcohol and violence, Dvoracek was dismissed from the team. His latest tirade involved a fight with a friend outside a bar in Norman, Oklahoma. Dvoracek gave his friend such a severe beating that he had to be hospitalized, and remained in intensive care for five days. Because of his inability to handle his alcohol-aggravated rage, Dvoracek's stellar college football career crashed and burned in flames of disgrace. His future football prospects remain uncertain and only time will tell if his life and career can be snatched from the clutches of alcohol.

Why do people allow themselves to be seduced by a substance capable of such death and destruction? I believe one of the major forces that perpetuates the drinking problem in our nation is the alcohol producers themselves. As they promote their deadly elixir, they don't tell the whole story. Their advertisements don't tell the stories of Natalie, Krystle, and Dusty—but my how they do advertise. According to the Tenth Special Report to the U.S. Congress on Alcohol and Health presented by the Secretary of Health and Human Services, in June 2000, alcohol producers spent $1.03 billion on advertising in the U.S. in 1996. From studies conducted in 2002 and 2003, the National Research Council Institute of Medicine and the Agricultural Marketing Service found that alcohol producers recently spent $1.6 billion advertising alcohol in the United States,[3] a 55 percent increase over the amount spent in 2000.

Much of this money is spent on television commercials. The

American Academy of Pediatrics reported in 1999 that the average young person sees approximately 2000 commercials advertising alcohol per year.[4] Although the occasional commercial encouraging them to drink responsibly or reminding them that friends don't let friends drive drunk will be shown, the Center on Alcohol Marketing and Youth reported in 2002 that underage youth, ages 12 to 20, were 128 times more likely to see a commercial promoting alcohol on television than an alcohol company-sponsored responsibility ad. They also found that these youth were 400 times more likely to see a promotional ad than an ad discouraging underage drinking and they were 188 times more likely to see an alcohol ad than one discouraging drinking and driving.[5]

All of these millions that alcohol companies spend on advertising is not wasted. According to the 2001 American Academy of Pediatrics article, "Alcohol Use and Abuse: A Pediatric Concern," 56 percent of students in grades 5–12 said that **alcohol** advertising encouraged them to drink. The article went on to state that with greater exposure to beer advertising, children have higher recall of brands or brand characters, are more likely to expect to drink as adults, and hold more positive beliefs about the social and ritual uses of beer.[6]

Alcohol advertisements are so persuasive because they are intentionally designed to be misleading. Have you noticed that they only show beautiful, happy people drinking alcohol and having a great time together? They never show the sadness and tragedy that often results from drinking. For instance, as Pete Coors stands in front of the snow-capped Colorado Rockies talking about how his beer is brewed from only pure, Rocky Mountain spring water, he doesn't tell the other side of the story. He doesn't mention the rivers of tears that are cried because of the devastation his beer causes. As we see a group of good ole' boys enjoying the great outdoors and hear them saying, "It doesn't get any better than this" on an Old Milwaukee beer commercial, you can bet we won't ever hear them talk about the misery that alcohol has dealt them. When the makers of Schlitz beer told us that we only go through life once so we better grab all the gusto we can, they did not tell us about the thousands and thousands of lives snuffed out by alcohol each year. When Budweiser takes us on a holiday sleigh ride through a winter wonderland, they never show us pictures of wrecked cars and mangled bodies from accidents caused by holiday drinking and driving. These commercials never show us drunks leaning over toilets throwing up. We never get to watch a clip of "the morning after" when the previous night's partier battles with an awful hangover just trying to make it through the day. They never let us see into the home of a couple screaming at each other as their marriage slowly dies one bottle at a time. They never show us a family and friends gathered around the grave of a loved one killed by a drunk driver. No, and they never will! The first alcohol company that tells the whole story will go bankrupt.

Sadly, stories like those of Natalie and Krystle are strangely missing from the steady stream of alcohol commercials flowing across our television screens. Even sadder still, stories like theirs are only the tip of an insidious iceberg floating just beneath the surface of our booze-flooded culture. Thousands are killed each year by the effects of alcohol leaving family and friends behind to pick up the pieces. Like an Oklahoma tornado, alcohol leaves a broad path of destruction with wrecked lives strewn across the cultural landscape of our nation. Few, if any of us, will remain untouched by the ravages of alcohol. This should be enough to cause everyone to avoid alcohol like the bubonic plague—but sadly, for many, it isn't.

Of course, alcohol's story is not a new one. It has a long and sordid tale. Its deceptive and destructive arms reach all of the way back to man's earliest days, making it the oldest and most used/abused drug in history. Dr. Sheldon Gottlieb, cardiologist at Johns Hopkins Bayview Medical Center in Baltimore, MD and Director of the Diabetes-Heart Failure Program at Johns Hopkins Health Care LLC, says, "Alcohol is a drug, the most widely available and the most widely consumed drug in our culture."[7] When Dr. Marvin Block was Chairman of the American Medical Association's Committee on Alcoholism, he commented: "Ours is a drug-oriented society, largely because of alcohol. Because of its social acceptance, alcohol is rarely thought of as a drug. But a drug it is, in scientific fact."[8] According to the National Institute on Alcohol Abuse and Alcoholism (NIAAA), alcohol presently wraps its long, deadly fingers around the throats of millions and millions of Americans who guzzle down its poisonous brew. It further traps a portion of those drinkers, approximately 14 million, in its death grip of alcohol abuse and alcoholism.[9] The cost of its negative impact on man's real happiness and productivity is incalculable. As we will see, Americans spend an incredible amount of money on alcohol each year and pay even more as they pick up the tab for cleaning up the mess that is left behind.

Chapter 3

Come on, it's only a drink!

"What's the big deal? It's only a drink," people say—but is that all it really is? Though I can't speak for everyone, I've always considered water, tea, coffee, milk, soft drinks, and the like when I've thought of drinks. It seems odd that anyone would consider something with the history of alcohol as "only a drink". What other drink can do what alcohol can do? What other drink has done what alcohol has done? When was the last time you heard of someone being killed in a car accident because the driver had consumed too many soft drinks? When was the last time you heard of someone losing his marriage or business because of his out of control milk drinking? How many times have you thrown up or had a hangover because you had too much tea to drink? Sounds ridiculous doesn't it? The truth is everyone knows that alcohol is much more than a drink. You don't have to have a Ph.D. in chemistry to know that. When compared to other drinks, alcohol is in a category all by itself.

Although you and I may take issue with someone's position on alcohol, and though we may debate the meaning, interpretation, or practical application of a particular alcohol-related passage of Scripture, the facts and figures don't lie. If we're going to fully comprehend the impact alcohol makes, we're going to have to consider those facts. But therein lies the problem—very few drinkers (and non-drinkers for that matter) ever take the time to study the facts. Many drinkers simply bury their heads in a can or glass of alcohol while other non-drinkers bury their heads in the sand of ignorance in a futile attempt to escape the truth. So, let's begin our investigation by taking a look at the price tag attached to alcohol and the economic impact it has on our lives and nation.

MAN, WHAT I WOULDN'T GIVE FOR A DRINK!

"He put that bottle to his head and pulled the trigger," so go the words of the popular song, "Whiskey Lullaby" performed by country music artist, Brad Paisley.[10] The song tells the sad story of a young man who drinks himself to death, grieving over a love gone bad. It's one of those traditional "crying in your beer" tear-jerkers that country music is so famous for. The really sad thing is that it tells the all-too-real story of many who really do kill themselves using a bottle as the weapon. Whether their deaths come slowly from years of drinking or instantaneously in some tragic incident, liquor drags millions of souls into an early grave.

Most of us are aware that drinking takes a devastating toll on American lives, but what we may not know is how much it costs us to drink. Although the true cost of alcohol abuse may never be known, studies consistently show that it costs us much more than we would ever want to pay.

Even though most Americans are careful when spending their money, when it comes to liquor, they seem willing to shell out lots of cold, hard cash. Recent reports show that alcohol sales are growing. Retail sales for beverage alcohol in 2002 were $137.2 billion which is a 6.3 percent increase over 2001 sales.[11] This breaks down to: 153 million cases of spirits, up for the fifth consecutive year, 241.6 million cases of wine, up for the ninth consecutive year, and 2.8 billion cases of beer, up for the seventh straight year.[12]

There's no denying it—Americans purchase massive amounts of alcohol every year. In fact, the University of Minnesota reported in 2002 that Americans age 14 and older consume an average of 2.75 gallons per person, per year.[13] In 2002, they forked over $137.2 billion of their hard-earned bucks for booze. But, people pay more than just the retail price for alcohol. For example, a

2003 article by the George Washington University Medical Center reported that the estimated cost to our nation's economy from accidents, health problems, crime, and lost productivity due to alcohol abuse is approximately $185 billion annually.[14] In contrast, according to the U.S. Census Bureau, the amount of excise taxes and license fees that were collected from the sale of alcohol in 2001 was approximately $4.5 billion.[15] That means that there was a $180.5 billion alcohol deficit for that year. In other words, the American economy lost $41.11 for every dollar the government collected from alcohol in 2001. Translating this into common English, that is equivalent to making an investment in a company in which, for every dollar invested, $41.11 is lost. I wonder how many would be interested in making an investment in such a company. Fact: alcohol always takes much more than it gives. (The Beer Institute, an industry trade group representing America's brewers claims that the alcohol industry contributes $144 billion to the U.S. economy per year.[16] Even if this is true, although I doubt it, this would still have created a $36.5 billion deficit for the year of 2001.)

Alcohol costs us in more ways than just in dollars and cents. When it comes to having a drink, it seems that no price is too high for many Americans—even if it costs them their lives. As they spend millions on alcohol, they seem unaware that they may be signing their own death warrants in the process. "The proof," one might say, "is in the proverbial bottle."

GOING, GOING, GONE

For starters, in April, 2004, the U.S. Surgeon General, Richard H. Carmona, M.D., stated that alcohol leads to more than 100,000 deaths each year in the United States.[17] A MSNBC news report on September 24, 2004 stated that excessive alcohol consumption is the third leading cause of preventable death in the U.S. and shortens the lives of these abusers by an average of 30 years.[18] According to MADD, alcohol kills 6.5 times more young people than all other illicit drugs combined.[19] Each year, thousands are killed in alcohol-related car and other types of accidents, hundreds are killed in alcohol-related crimes, and thousands die from alcohol-related diseases. The National Center for Health Statistics states that alcohol is a factor in about 30 percent of all completed suicides each year in America.[20] A *Current Health 2* article entitled, "Suicide: what causes someone to commit suicide—and what can you do about it?" states that alcohol is a factor in over half of all youth suicides.[21] In addition, the University of Minnesota reported in 2002 that 80 percent of all adolescent suicides have been reported to be children of alcoholic parents.[22] Since depression is the primary cause of suicide for all ages, it seems rather ridiculous and tragic that an already depressed person would consume a drug that is a depressant.

Alcohol also has a huge negative impact on the collective physical health of Americans. The Community Health Improvement Partners' "2001 Community Health Needs Assessment" stated that approximately 40% of all admissions to our nation's hospitals each year are alcohol related.[23] A Sept. 24, 2004 MSNBC news report noted that, according to the Centers for Disease Control (CDC), an estimated 34,833 people in 2001 died from cirrhosis of the liver, cancer, and other diseases linked to drinking too much beer, wine, and spirits.[24] The disease that most affects heavy drinkers is liver disease and the U.S. Department of Health and Human Services reports that over 2 million Americans suffer from alcohol-related liver disease and that 10 to 20 percent of heavy drinkers will develop alcoholic cirrhosis.[25] The CDC reported that in 2001, 27,035 people died of cirrhosis alone.[26] Heavy drinkers are also at greater risk for high blood pressure, stroke, heart disease, cancer, and pancreatitis. U.S. government researchers discovered that the number of American adults who abuse alcohol or are alcohol dependent rose to 17.6 million in 2001–2002 (slightly more than 8 percent of the population)—up from 13.8 million in 1991–1992 (slightly more than 7 percent of the population),[27] increasing the potential for alcohol-related illnesses in America.

Because some alcohol abusers often participate in high-risk sexual behavior, they have an increased risk of contracting and spreading venereal diseases as well. Statistically, heavy drinkers often have multiple sex partners so they have a much higher probability of contracting and spreading the deadly HIV virus.[28]

In addition to the risks just mentioned, because of the way their bodies metabolize alcohol, women who drink, also have a 41 percent greater risk of developing breast cancer.[29] When women who are pregnant drink, they significantly endanger their unborn babies. The National Center for Chronic Disease Prevention and Health Promotion warns:

- The adverse health effects that are associated with alcohol-exposed pregnancies include miscarriage, premature delivery, low birth weight, Sudden Infant Death Syndrome (SIDS), and prenatal alcohol-related conditions (e.g., Fetal Alcohol Syndrome (FAS) and alcohol-related neurodevelopmental disorders).
- Alcohol-related neurodevelopmental disorder and alcohol-related birth defects are believed to occur approximately three times as often as FAS.
- Fetal Alcohol Syndrome is one of the leading causes of mental retardation, and is directly attributable to drinking during pregnancy. FAS is characterized by growth retardation, facial abnormalities, and central nervous system dysfunction (i.e., learning disabilities and lower IQ), as well as behavioral problems.
- The incidence of FAS in the U.S. ranges from 0.2 to 1.5 per 1,000 live births.
- Any maternal alcohol use in the periconceptional period (i.e., during the three months before pregnancy or during the first trimester) is associated with a six-fold increased risk of SIDS.
- Binge drinking (five or more drinks at a time) during a mother's first trimester of pregnancy is associated with an eight-fold increase in the odds that the infant will die of SIDS.[30]

Billy Sunday, the great evangelist, once said:

"If hydrophobia produced one millionth part of the disease and trouble the saloon causes, every dog in America would be killed off before Monday morning."[31]

WHERE THE RUBBER MEETS THE ROAD

According to the U.S. Department of Transportation, National Highway Traffic Safety Administration (NHTSA), 17,013 people (like Natalie and Krystle) were killed on America's highways in alcohol-related car crashes in 2003.[32] This number represents 40 percent of total traffic fatalities for the year. This means that there was an average of one alcohol-related fatality every 31 minutes in 2003. In addition to this number, approximately 275,000 people were injured in crashes in which officials reported that alcohol was present.[33] This translates into an average of one person being injured by an alcohol-related accident almost every 2 minutes.

To put these numbers into perspective, consider September 11, 2001. When terrorists attacked our country by flying airliners into buildings, we were stunned. We couldn't believe that such a tragedy could occur right here in our own nation. The death count was staggering—almost 3000, including those confirmed dead, reported dead, and reported missing. The public outcry for retaliation was deafening and, as President Bush promised, our nation reacted with a great show of force against the perpetrators. What is amazing is that the number of people killed in 2003 by alcohol-related car crashes alone (many more deaths occurred from other alcohol-related incidents) was almost six times the number killed on 9/11. Yet where is the public outrage? Why have we not declared war on those perpetrators?

Every time a commercial airliner crashes, the news agencies are all over the story. Images of plane wreckage cover our television screens for days. There are investigations and inquiries. Try to imagine what would happen if there were four or five such crashes each month. The 17,013 people killed in alcohol-related car crashes per year is equivalent to 4–5 airplanes carrying 300 passengers each crashing every month. Imagine how great the national outcry would be if this were to happen. Most likely every airplane in the nation would be grounded.

Consider these figures:

- The number killed by alcohol in America each year is approximately the same as the 103,000 killed when we dropped the atomic bombs on the Japanese cities of Hiroshima and Nagasaki.
- During the Korean War (1950–1953), tragically, over 54,000 American soldiers died. But this number is only one-half of the number killed by alcohol each year. Over the three years that the Korean War was being fought, more than 300,000 Americans were killed by alcohol.
- During the Vietnam War (1964–1973), regrettably, over 58,000 American soldiers died. But this number is only slightly more than one-half of the people who die from alcohol-related causes each year. Over the years that the Vietnam War was being fought, more than 900,000 Americans were killed by alcohol.

Our country spends huge amounts of money each year attempting to stop illicit drug traffic, but we do relatively little to curb the use of alcohol. Why? We forced cigarette companies to stop advertising on television, why haven't we done the same to alcohol companies? Of course, there are numerous reasons why no massive action has been taken against alcohol—let me suggest a few:

1. Alcohol is too socially acceptable and people don't want to give it up.
2. Alcohol is not seen by the public as the destructive substance it really is.

3. There is too much money to be made from the sale of alcohol.

4. The church is, for the most part, strangely silent on the issue.

Surprisingly, even though they are exposed to a continual onslaught of alcohol hype, average Americans are clearly aware of the potential threat that alcohol poses to them. In a 2001 survey conducted by the Gallup Organization on the general driving age public, 97 percent felt that drinking and driving was a threat to their personal safety and 66 percent felt that it was extremely important to do something to reduce the problem.[34] Their concern is founded on fact. The NHTSA found in 2001 that about three in every ten Americans (30%) will be involved in an alcohol-related crash at some time in their lives.[35]

Drinking and driving has become such a problem in our nation that it has become the most frequently committed violent crime.[36] NHTSA reported that 1.5 million drivers were arrested in 2002 for driving under the influence of alcohol or narcotics which is an arrest rate of 1 for every 130 licensed drivers in the U.S.[37] According to MADD (Mothers Against Drunk Driving), beer is the drink most commonly consumed by those who are stopped for alcohol-impaired driving or who are involved in alcohol-related crashes. In fact, according to Jeffrey W. Runge, M.D., Administrator of the Department of Transportation, beer is involved 80 percent of the time and liquor and wine are involved 20 percent of the time.[38]

To confirm how correct these numbers are, a few days ago during my daily three mile run I noticed the large number of beer bottles and cans along the 1½ mile stretch of road south of my home. Out of curiosity my wife and I decided to perform a little experiment. We walked the 1½ miles and counted the containers—she counted the soft drink cans and bottles (including colas, health drinks, milk, etc.) and I counted the beer cans and bottles. Although we expected to find more beer containers than soft drink containers, we did not expect the numbers to be so disproportionate. Here are the results of our experiment: we counted 152 soft drink containers and 455 beer containers—a 3 to 1 ratio. Even though this experiment was not scientific, I believe it does confirm the fact that many people *do* regularly consume beer while driving.

According to the U.S. Department of Transportation, officials determine if an accident is alcohol-related by the following criteria:

> "a motor vehicle crash is considered to be alcohol-related if at least one driver or non-occupant (such as a pedestrian or pedalcyclist) involved in the crash is determined to have had a Blood Alcohol Concentration (BAC) of 0.01 gram per deciliter (g/dl) or higher. Thus, any fatality that occurs in an alcohol-related crash is considered an alcohol-related fatality. In most states it is a criminal offense to operate a motor vehicle at a BAC of 0.08 g/dl or above. The greatest numbers of offenders who were involved in fatal car crashes with a BAC of 0.08 g/dl were those between the ages of 21 and 34. Those aged 21–24 years accounted for 32 percent of the fatal crashes, those aged 25–34 years accounted for 27 percent, and those aged 35–44 years accounted for 24 percent."[39]

Sadly, younger people are the worst drinking and driving offenders in our nation—literally approaching epidemic proportions. It is so unfortunate that the most vulnerable of our society are the primary victims of this culprit.

HE'S IN THE JAILHOUSE NOW

By now, it should be of no surprise that alcohol is closely linked with violence. The U.S. Bureau of Justice tells us that more violent crimes are committed under the influence of alcohol than are by all other drugs.[40] A 2001 Boston University of Public Health study indicates that alcohol encourages aggressive behavior in drinkers by disrupting the normal brain mechanisms that restrain impulsive actions such as aggression.[41] Of course, if you've ever been around people who are drinking heavily, you know this is true. The National Center for Chronic Disease Prevention and Health Promotion provides the following alarming facts:

- 40% of all crimes (violent and non-violent) were committed under the influence of alcohol.
- 40% of convicted rape and sexual assault offenders said that they were drinking at the time of their crime.
- Two-thirds of victims of domestic violence reported that alcohol was involved in the incident.
- Nearly one-half of the cases of child abuse and neglect are associated with parental alcohol or drug abuse.[42]

In addition, the University of Minnesota reports that 55 to 75 percent of homicide victims had been drinking at the time of the incident and that 70 percent of adult female alcoholics were sexually abused as children.[43]

The National Institute on Alcohol Abuse and Alcoholism (NIAAA) reports that drinking on American college campuses produces the following victimizations each year:

- 600,000 students are assaulted by another student.
- 110,000 students are arrested for an alcohol-related violation.
- 70,000 are sexually assaulted.

Bellarmine University in Louisville, Kentucky, found that 95 percent of violent crime, 90 percent of all reported rapes, and 80 percent of all vandalism on college campuses are alcohol-related.[44]

Ironically, as we spend millions prosecuting criminals, trying to reduce crime, and attempting to rehabilitate felons, we essentially ignore one of the primary causes of crime—alcohol. Although our government makes some effort to enforce the laws regulating alcohol, these laws for the most part, deal primarily with the effects of alcohol abuse—not its prevention. All the while, alcohol floods over our society as if a dam has broken upstream.

WHY DO THEY DO IT?

The obvious question is, "Why do they do it?" Why do Americans put a substance like alcohol into their bodies knowing it has the potential of doing them such harm? How do they rationalize it?

Drinkers frequently give three excuses for drinking:

- *"Everybody is doing it."* (A response to peer pressure and the desire to fit in.)
- *"It's an adult beverage."* (A belief that adults can handle their liquor and deal with its effects.)
- *"It helps me to relax."* (A common misconception that alcohol provides an escape from problems.)

"BEER" PRESSURE!

"Everybody's doing it!" What parent hasn't heard these words coming from the mouth of his child at one time or another? When I used this line on my father, he would always say, "If everyone was jumping off of a cliff, would you jump too?" Of course, I always said no, because in my heart, I knew his reasoning was right. Strangely enough, though, this is the very excuse many use when drinking. Surely they must know that even if everyone *is* doing it, that's still not a good enough reason—especially when it comes to drinking.

Although many adults are vulnerable to this line of thinking, unfortunately, as we have seen, adolescents are most vulnerable. "Beer" (peer) pressure exerts an unbelievable force on them. The U.S. Department of Health and Human Services reports that "beer" pressure begins early in the lives of young people; 33 percent of 4th graders and more than 50 percent of 6th graders say they have been pressured by friends to drink alcohol.[45] If they become convinced that they have to drink to fit in, they will. Among the leading reasons adolescents give for drinking, finding acceptance among their peers is near the top. Regrettably, millions give in to this pressure.

The U.S. Department of Health and Human Services and the American Medical Association reported in 2002 and 2003, that of the some 109 million Americans aged 12 or older who drank alcohol about 11 million were underage drinkers.[46] The U.S. Department of Health and Human Services went on to say that out of those 11 million underage drinkers, 7.2 million binge drank.[47] The American Academy of Pediatrics tells us that the average age that children begin drinking is 11 years for boys and 13 years for girls.[48] Actually, this shouldn't shock any of us. As I have already cited, the average American youth views approximately 2000 commercials promoting alcohol every year.[49] With a constant bombardment like this, it is no wonder that so many are drinking. A study by the National Center on Addiction and Substance Abuse at Columbia University in 2003 found that what is so alarming about underage drinking is that children who begin drinking before age 21 are more than twice as likely to develop alcohol-related problems and those who begin drinking before age 15 are four times more likely to become alcoholics than those who do not drink before age 21.[50]

The 2004 *Monitoring the Future Study*, conducted by the University of Michigan, found:

- Alcohol has been tried by 44 percent of eighth graders, 64 percent of tenth graders, and 77 percent of twelfth graders; active use is also widespread.
- 20 percent of eighth graders have been drunk at least once.
- 11 percent of eighth graders, 22 percent of tenth graders, and 29 percent of twelfth graders drank heavily (over five drinks in one sitting) in the two weeks preceding a national alcohol survey.[51]

Even more tragic, as we have already seen, is the fact that alcohol kills over six times more young people than all other illicit drugs combined. And yet, ironically, we hear much more about stopping illicit drug usage than we do about curbing alcohol use. In the end, the final bill that underage drinking racks up in our nation is estimated at more than $53 billion per year.[52]

Although it is illegal for the underaged to purchase alcohol, they obviously find ways to get their hands on it. The U.S. Department of Health and Human Services says that 75 percent of 8th graders and 89 percent of 10th graders believe that alcohol is readily available to them.[53] Whether they find someone older to purchase it for them or they falsify their ages and buy it themselves, the fact is: they are getting the liquor.

I've got to ask, "Where in the world are these kids' parents?" A 1999 Peter Hart Poll may help answer that question. It found that one fourth (25%) of the parents of 9th-12th graders said they would allow their children to attend a party where they suspected alcohol would be used.[54] So apparently, these particular parents think nothing of underage drinking.It appears that not only are they doing nothing to prevent it, some parents are actually allowing, or worse yet, encouraging their children to drink by their own indifference and/or drinking habits. These parents either ignore or are woefully ignorant of the fact that alcohol is extremely destructive, especially to young people. Not only are their bodies more vulnerable to the detrimental effects of alcohol, but most underage drinkers greatly overestimate their ability to handle the intoxicating effects of alcohol, thus placing themselves at greater risk for disaster. Like sitting ducks, they become vulnerable to the aberrant behavior it produces. For example: they are very apt to drink and drive and they think nothing of riding in a vehicle driven by someone who has been drinking; youth who drink are more apt to use tobacco and other types of drugs, and because alcohol has the power to lower their moral inhibitions, they engage in sex more often, thus increasing their chances of producing an unwanted pregnancy or contracting a venereal disease. The American Academy of Pediatrics warns that those ages 14 and 15 who use alcohol are 4 and 7 times more likely, respectively, to have sexual intercourse as their peers who do not consume alcohol. They also found that these 15-year-olds who do drink have as many as 4 sexual partners.[55]

What is more disturbing is the fact that drinking among college students is even worse. According to Mark S. Goldman, Ph.D., Associate Director of the NIAAA, "available research indicates that approximately 80% of college students drink and that half of college student drinkers engage in heavy episodic drinking."[56] Numerous studies have found that college students across America spend billions more each year on alcohol than they do on books and all other soft drinks combined. In 1997, Harvard University found that 52 percent of college students drank to get drunk, compared to 39 percent in 1993.[57] According to this same study, two in five American college students binge drink.[58] (Binge drinking is defined as drinking five or more drinks at a time).

This amount of drinking has devastating effects on these students. Dr. Goldman adds,

> "Excessive alcohol intake among college students is associated with a variety of adverse consequences: fatal and nonfatal injuries; alcohol poisoning; blackouts; academic failure; violence, including rape and assault; unintended pregnancy; sexually transmitted diseases, including HIV/AIDS; property damage; and vocational and criminal consequences that could jeopardize future job prospects."[59]

Drinking is at its worst among students who are in fraternities and sororities. In 1999, Drug Strategies reported that four in five resident (80%) members were binge drinkers, compared to two in five (40%) students in the general college population. This fact is leading the fraternity and sorority organizations to rethink their policies on alcohol.[60] According to *The Oklahoman,* Omar Zantout, an OU student and president of the University of Oklahoma Interfraternity Council, said that alcohol is extremely accessible at frat houses. "There are those who get out of high school and have a freedom they have never had before," Zantout said. "They go wild and fall into the category of binge drinking."[61]

As I write this chapter, news agencies continue reporting

the story of the death of a 19-year-old student at the University of Oklahoma who died from acute alcohol poisoning. The student, a Sigma Chi pledge, was found dead in the Sigma Chi fraternity house Thursday morning, Sept. 30, 2004, after a fraternity function the previous night. News agencies are reporting that at the time of his death, he had a 0.42 BAC which is five times the legal limit. Presumably, he was binge drinking at a frat party. According to *The Oklahoman,* a 150 lb. man would need to drink approximately eighteen shots of 100-proof cinnamon schnapps in three hours, or twenty-four 12-ounce glasses of 3.2 beer in three hours, or fourteen 5-ounce glasses of wine in three hours to reach a BAC of 0.42.[62] Sadly, during this same week, two other college students in other states died from the same cause. Unfortunately, these students have become three more tragic statistics on a long list of students who have binged themselves to death.

So how many college students are killed by alcohol abuse each year? On April 10, 2002, *The News Hour with Jim Lehrer,* aired a report entitled, "Binge Drinking", addressing this issue.[63] On that program, Susan Dentzer reported that a federally-funded study found that alcohol consumption and resulting accidents are responsible for approximately 1,400 deaths to college students per year. Quoting Ralph Hingson of the Boston University School of Public Health, Dentzer reported that, in addition to those who are killed, an estimated 500,000 students between the ages of 18 and 24 are unintentionally injured each year while under the influence of alcohol. More than 600,000 students are assaulted by other students who have been drinking. An estimated 400,000 students a year have unprotected sex while drinking and approximately 70,000 are victims of date rape. More than 100,000 say they were too drunk to know whether the sex they had was consensual or not. Continuing to quote Hingson, Dentzer said that an estimated 2,000,000 college students drink and drive and approximately 3,000,000 students ride in an automobile driven by someone who has been drinking. Dentzer went on to say that Hingson and his colleagues believe that all of these estimates are conservative—meaning that the actual numbers are probably much worse.

In addition to these findings, the *Harvard College Alcohol Study* conducted between 1993 and 1997 found that college athletes were more likely to drink heavily than other college students. In fact, these researchers found that almost two-thirds (66%) of male college athletes were binge drinkers.[64] A similar study in 1997 found that half (50%) of female college athletes were also binge drinkers.[65]

It has become almost impossible these days to keep track of all the news reports of the alcohol-related tragedies in our nation—especially on college campuses. The following news report by the Associated Press that appeared in *The Oklahoman* is all too familiar:

> "STEAMBOAT SPRINGS, Colo.–A 24-year-old Colorado Mountain College student died of heart and lung failure because of alcohol poisoning, according to a toxicology report.
>
> Joseph Michael Osborne's body was found at an off-campus house Oct. 27. Osborne had a blood alcohol content of 0.302, more than three times the legal limit, Routt County Coroner Rob Ryg said.
>
> Osborne had been drinking at a bar with acquaintances. His death is at least the fifth alcohol-related death of a Colorado college student.
>
> On Oct. 21, 20-year-old Amanda Morrison of Clifton Park, N.Y., had a blood alcohol level of 0.22 when she fell out of a dormitory window at Colorado College in Colorado Springs.
>
> Samantha Spady, 19, of Beatrice, Neb., died of alcohol poisoning Sept. 5 after consuming at least 30 drinks in 11 hours. She was found in a fraternity house near Colorado State in Fort Collins.
>
> Lynn Gordon Bailey Jr., 18, of Dallas was found dead at a fraternity house near the University of Colorado campus in Boulder 11 days later. He died of alcohol poisoning after a fraternity ritual.
>
> Preliminary tests indicate Jason Bannick, 19, of Centennial had alcohol in his system when he was struck and killed Oct. 24 by an SUV

while walking in the middle of a highway near Durango. He was a sophomore at Fort Lewis College in Colorado."[66]

It is obvious that many are drowning in a sea of alcohol, dying by the hundreds. How can anyone say that alcohol is just another drink when the equivalent of two atomic bombs (Hiroshima & Nagasaki), are exploding in our nation through a bottle, killing over 100,000 each year?

WHISKEY FOR MY MEN, AND BEER FOR MY HORSES

When attempting to justify their drinking, drinkers use an arsenal of arguments. While young people use the "everybody's doing it" excuse, many adults use the "it's just an adult beverage" excuse. The argument goes something like this: a legal, consenting adult is capable of making an informed decision about drinking and should have the right to use alcohol any time, any place—regardless of the consequences.

To help bolster this argument, popular singers such as country performer Toby Keith sing songs like, "Whiskey for my men and beer for my horses,"[67] that conjure up images of rough and rowdy cowboys, real men, who ride into town in a cloud of dust with their six-guns a blazin' and then make their way to the nearest saloon to 'belly-up' to the bar for a drink. What real man can't relate with that?

If we believe the macho malarkey that we hear in songs or that we see in movies and beer commercials, then we'll believe that to be real men or women we have to drink—and drink a lot! According to many of the messages in the media, if we don't drink, we're either duds who wouldn't know a good time if it hit us in the face or we're tin horns who couldn't fight our way out of a wet paper sack even if our lives depended on it. Either way, we're losers.

Apparently lines of reasoning like this are effective because approximately 100 million adults in America drink. Even though most are convinced that they can handle their liquor, the evidence says otherwise. For example, of these 100 million adult drinkers, 14 million qualify as alcohol abusers or alcoholics.[68] Additionally, the CDC found that approximately 33 percent of these 100 million adult drinkers binge drink.[69] In addition, a 1998 NIAAA study found that drinking adults are the primary cause of such workplace problems as absenteeism, tardiness, and poor quality of work. They also cost their employers billions of dollars in lost productivity each year.[70] This is in addition to all of the other carnage alcohol brings on our nation through such things as: alcohol-induced illnesses, the wreckage of drinking and driving, alcohol-induced crime, etc.

These tough, hard-drinking guys and gals are also a major contributor to such national problems as divorce, broken homes and the resulting psychological damage to children, ruined reputations, bankruptcies, destroyed businesses, etc.—costs that are simply impossible to assess. Hardly the report card we would expect from those who can "handle their liquor."

BUT IT HELPS ME TO ESCAPE FROM MY PROBLEMS

"It's someone else's fault."

"My mother didn't love me."

"My father wasn't around enough when I was growing up."

"I never got a fair chance in school."

"My teachers were against me."

"No one at work will give me a break."

"The government isn't helping me like it should."

It's true—all of us have problems. It could be that some of these things happened to you and you really weren't to blame. Whether this is true or not, attempting to cover up or solve these problems with alcohol is never the answer. This "run-from-my-problems" philosophy is a major problem in our culture. Few are willing to take responsibility for their actions. Of course, there's nothing new about that. Go back to the Garden of Eden, and you'll find Eve blaming the serpent and Adam blaming Eve. Today, we are playing the same game. Escapism is the *motis operandi* of our age. School teachers, ministers, and others in similar professions are constantly confronted with parents who refuse to take responsibility for their children or who refuse to make their children take responsibility for themselves. Over the 20+ years I've been a pastor, I've had parents blame me, the church, the youth minister, or anyone else they could find for their child's problems. I remember one mother in particular who wrote a letter informing our youth minister and me that we were both going to burn in Hell because her daughter was sent to prison for grand theft auto. Although we had tried to help the young lady, she refused our counsel, so how in the world could we have kept her out of jail? Yet, her mother blamed us for her daughter's problems. (Apparently she never considered the possibility that she and her husband could have been a major part of the problem.) Like many, she believed that if she could pin-the-blame on someone else, she'd be exonerated. Unfortunately it just doesn't work that way. Eventually, the consequences of our actions catch up with us. Paul emphasized this fact when he wrote,

> "Don't be misled. Remember that you can't ignore God and get away with it. You will always reap what you sow!" Ephesians 6:7, NLT

I believe that it's this same escapist philosophy that contributes greatly to the alcohol-crazed culture we live in today. Way back in the 1960s, Dr. Marvin Block stated, "Alcoholism is an attempt to escape reality by the use of a socially accepted drug."[71] Many deceive themselves into believing that if they can forget their problems for a little while, things might get better. As a result they drown their problems with booze in a feeble attempt to escape from reality. Sadly, alcohol normally only complicates their problems and makes things worse. If their problems are financial, by drinking they simply dig a deeper hole by spending money they can't spare for booze they don't need. If their problems are at home, by drinking all they do is make things worse by wasting time at the bar instead of spending time at home working on their problems.

If their problem is at work, alcohol won't fix that either. This is why Solomon warned:

> "Do not carouse with drunkards and gluttons, for they are on their way to poverty." Proverbs 23:20–21, NLT

We might like to believe that people in an "enlightened" society like ours would know that escapism isn't a logical, sane way of dealing with life's problems, but unfortunately many abandon all logic when it comes to drinking. Thomas Trotter, physician to the British Navy, implied this when he wrote in his "Essay on Drunkenness" in 1804: "The habit of drunkenness is a disease of the mind."[72] Simply stated, people who try to live in an alcohol-induced, make-believe, escapist world are not in their right minds. Those who attempt to escape through a bottle should listen to what Solomon wrote centuries ago:

> "Wine is a mocker and beer a brawler; whoever is led astray by them is not wise." Proverbs 20:1, NIV

According to the Bible, believing that an answer can be found at the bottom of a bottle is the thinking of a fool.

Billy Sunday, the former professional baseball player and ex-heavy drinker who became a Christian evangelist early in the 20th century, took a strong stand against the evils of alcohol. In his famous sermon, "Booze," he said:

> "The saloon is a liar. It promises good cheer and sends sorrow. It promises health and causes disease. It promises prosperity and sends adversity. It promises happiness and sends misery. Yes, it sends the husband home with a lie on his lips to his wife; and the boy home with a lie on his lips to his mother; and it causes the employee to lie to his employer. It degrades. It is God's worst enemy and the devil's best friend. It spares neither youth nor old age. It is waiting with a dirty blanket for the baby to crawl into the world. It lies in wait for the unborn . . . The saloon comes as near being a rat hole for a wage-earner to dump his wages in as anything you can find. The only interest it pays is red eyes and foul breath, and the loss of health. You can go in with money and you come out with empty pockets. You go in with character and you come out ruined. You go in with a good position and you lose it. You lose

your position at the bank, or in the cab of the locomotive. And it pays nothing back but disease and damnation and gives an extra dividend in delirium tremens and a free pass to hell. And then it will let your wife be buried in the potter's field, and your children go to the asylum, and yet you walk out and say the saloon is a good institution, when it is the dirtiest thing on earth. It hasn't one leg to stand on and has nothing to commend it to a decent man, not one thing."[73]

Even if alcohol is limited to adult consumption, why would anyone want to play Russian roulette with it—especially when considering its great potential to cripple and kill? How could anyone believe that something as destructive as alcohol is "just another drink"? Insisting that alcohol is "just another drink" is like saying a nuclear bomb is "just another explosive".

Dr. Willard Brewing, writing in *The Church Herald,* summed it up pretty well:

"The liquor business is the only business I know that keeps a one-sided ledger—that details with receipts and ignores legitimate expenditures. It takes the profits and leaves the expenses to someone else. Within one year in Vancouver I buried three young people who had been killed by alcohol on the highways. That is not my assumption; that is the verdict of the jury. At not one of those funerals was there a representative of the business that killed them. They did not pay the funeral expenses or look after the orphans. If it had been a railway accident, the fault of the road, they would have been there. Had it happened in an industrial plant, they would have been there. But this accursed business grasps its privileges but takes no stock in its obligations. Some foolish people seem to think it pays. If it met its legitimate bills, it would go bankrupt in a year."[74]

$\mathcal{B}$ EER ON THE BRAIN

"O God, that men should put an enemy in their mouths to steal away their brains! That we should with joy, pleasance, revel, and applause transform ourselves into beasts!" William Shakespeare, *Othello*. ACT II, Scene 3

A little known fact is that alcohol (of all kinds) is poisonous to our bodies and in large enough amounts, can kill us. Different types of alcohol attack different parts of the body. For instance, wood alcohol attacks the optical nerves sometimes causing permanent blindness. Isopropyl alcohol, commonly known as rubbing alcohol, if ingested, can cause irritation of the mucous membranes and eyes, gastric hemorrhaging, vomiting, respiratory depression, and even comas. Beverage alcohol, though damaging to numerous parts of the body, primarily attacks the brain, liver, pancreas, stomach, and small intestine.

To understand why alcohol can be so damaging, we must understand how it works in the body. Alcohol affects each person differently. While some individuals are intoxicated after only one drink, others can consume large quantities before they begin to show any signs of intoxication. Since women metabolize alcohol differently than men, they are affected more quickly and by smaller amounts of alcohol than are men. In addition, according to the Insurance Institute for Highway Safety (IIHS), the effects of alcoholic drinks vary greatly because their rate of absorption and the blood alcohol content (BAC) attained varies from person to person due to such factors as weight, amount of fat tissue, and stomach contents.[75] IIHS goes on to say that a person's level of impairment is not determined by the type of drink, but rather by the amount of alcohol ingested over a specific period of time.[76]

The National Highway Traffic Safety Administration (NHTSA) defines a standard drink as 12 ounces of beer, 5 ounces of wine (9 oz. wine cooler), or 1.5 ounces of 80-proof distilled spirits which all contain the same amount of alcohol.[77] So, how much alcohol is too much? According to the NHTSA chart below, if a person drinks more than this, he is putting himself at risk for illness and/or injury.[78]

	Drinks per Week	Drinks per Occasion
Men	14	4
Women	7	3
Age 65+	7	3

A common misconception about alcohol that causes confusion is the belief that a drinker is not significantly affected by alcohol if he/she doesn't show visible signs of drunkenness. In fact, the IIHS says:

> "Many alcohol-impaired drivers do not appear drunk in the traditional way. Research has shown that even small amounts of alcohol can impair the skills involved in driving. The persistent notion that the problem is predominantly one of drunk drivers has allowed many drinking drivers to decide they are not part of the problem."[79]

Keeping in mind that the legal BAC is less than 0.08, the following information from the IIHS is startling and illustrates how a person does not have to have a BAC of 0.08 or higher to be significantly impaired:

> "At a BAC as low as 0.02 percent alcohol affects driving ability and crash likelihood. The probability of a crash begins to increase significantly at 0.05 percent BAC and climbs rapidly after about 0.08 percent. For drivers aged 35 and older with a BAC at or above 0.15 percent on weekend nights, the likelihood of being killed in a single-vehicle crash is more than 380 times higher than it is for non-drinking drivers."[80]

Although many believe alcohol is a stimulant, it is actually a depressant. It is believed to be a stimulant because drinkers seem to be stimulated, but it only *appears* that way. In fact, their body systems are being systematically shut down by alcohol—not revved up. To quote Dr. Michaele Dunlap:

> "Speech becomes free and animated, social inhibitions may be forgotten, and the drinker can begin to act and feel more emotional. But these effects are misleading; the 'stimulation' occurs only because alcohol affects those portions of the brain that control judgment. 'Being stimulated' by alcohol actually amounts to a depression of self-control."[81]

As a depressant, alcohol works much like an anesthetic. The moment it enters the body, it begins to irritate the lining of the mouth and esophagus creating a numbing effect. Because alcohol has a high affinity for water, it easily travels throughout the body and particularly affects those organs that contain large quantities of water and need large supplies of blood—organs such as the brain and liver.[82] As alcohol moves through the digestive system, about 20 percent is absorbed in the stomach and 80 percent in the small intestine.[83] As it enters the bloodstream, absorption occurs relatively quickly causing the drinker to begin to feel its effects in mere minutes.

The first organ to be significantly affected by alcohol is the brain. Alcohol initially anesthetizes the brain and then, as additional amounts of alcohol reach the brain, permanent cell damage begins to occur. For some time, it has been known that chronic alcohol abuse causes brain volume loss, but a new study by Johns Hopkins University in Baltimore suggests that even **moderate** alcohol intake may promote brain atrophy.[84] The American Heart Association says that alcohol-related brain atrophy may be associated with lower cognition and reduced extremity function and there is a strong correlation between heavy drinking and a higher risk of stroke and brain deterioration.[85]

Obviously, the amount and strength of the alcohol consumed will determine exactly how much the brain will be affected, but even in small concentrations, alcohol has a negative effect on the brain. This fact alone makes underage drinking an extremely serious issue. Because the brain continues to develop throughout adolescence and into young adulthood, young people are more vulnerable to permanent brain damage from alcohol than are adults.[86]

The clumsy, awkward actions typical of those who have been drinking are not as funny and harmless as they may appear. According to Dr. Dunlap:

> " . . . these actions are produced by an effect called 'blood-sludging'. This occurs when the alcohol content causes the red blood cells to clump together causing the small blood vessels to plug up, starving the tissues of oxygen, ultimately causing death of the cell. This cell death is most serious, and often most unrecognized, in the brain. As these cells are affected or killed, outward signs such as slurred speech and clumsiness are evidenced. With this increased pressure created by blood-sludging, capillaries break, causing red eyes in the morning, or the red, blotchy skin seen on the heavy drinker's face. Blood vessels can also break in the stomach and esophagus leading to hemorrhage, or even death."[87]

When a person's rate of drinking exceeds his/her body's ability to eliminate alcohol, the BAC begins to increase. A healthy adult body can eliminate approximately ½ to ¾ ounces of alcohol per hour. This is the equivalent of 1 ounce of 100-proof whiskey, one large beer, or about 3 to 4 ounces of wine.[88] Contrary to what we may have heard, it is impossible to speed up the elimination of alcohol from the body. According to the BBC article, "Alcohol Awareness: The Effect on the Body," only time will sober a person up—drinking strong coffee, exercising, or taking a cold shower will not help.[89]

As the alcohol level in the blood continues to rise, the drinker's silly actions, clumsy reflexes, and slurred speech begin to give way to more serious symptoms. The slowing effect that alcohol has on the muscles, including the heart, begins to paralyze the systems in the body. When the BAC reaches 0.30 to 0.40, the drinker may go into a coma and when it reaches 0.50 to 0.60, death normally occurs. The following chart by Intoximeters Inc. shows how alcohol affects the brain at various levels of blood alcohol content[90]:

STAGES OF ALCOHOL INTOXICATION

BAC (g/100 ml of blood or g/210 ml of breath)	Stage	Clinical symptoms
0.01 - 0.05	Sub clinical	Behavior nearly normal by ordinary observation
0.03 - 0.12	Euphoria	Mild euphoria, sociability, talkativeness Increased self-confidence; decreased inhibitions Diminution of attention, judgment, and control Beginning of sensory-motor impairment Loss of efficiency in finer performance tests
0.09 - 0.25	Excitement	Emotional instability; loss of critical judgment Impairment of perception, memory, and comprehension Decreased sensatory response; increased reaction time Reduced visual acuity, peripheral vision, and glare recovery Sensory-motor in-coordination; impaired balance Drowsiness
0.18 - 0.30	Confusion	Disorientation, mental confusion; dizziness Exaggerated emotional states Disturbances of vision and of perception of color, form, motion, and dimensions Increased pain threshold Increased muscular in-coordination; staggering gait; slurred speech Apathy, lethargy
0.25 - 0.40	Stupor	General inertia; approaching loss of motor functions Markedly decreased response to stimuli Marked muscular in-coordination; inability to stand or walk Vomiting; incontinence Impaired consciousness; sleep or stupor
0.35 - 0.50	Coma	Complete unconsciousness Depressed or abolished reflexes Subnormal body temperature Incontinence Impairment of circulation and respiration Possible death
0.45 +	Death	Death from respiratory arrest

According to the Michigan State University fact sheet entitled "Basic Alcohol Information," when enough of the vital centers of the brain have been depressed by alcohol, unconsciousness occurs. Additionally, the amount of alcohol that it takes to produce unconsciousness is dangerously close to a fatal dose and people who survive alcohol poisoning sometimes suffer irreversible brain damage.[91] The MSU fact sheet goes on to warn students of another life-threatening aspect of drinking to the point of unconsciousness—choking to death on vomit. Vomiting is the body's way of protecting itself from too much alcohol; unfortunately, it sometimes causes death because it often occurs when the person is unconscious and is incapable of keeping his airway clear.[92]

Spiritually, I think it is significant that the ability to make moral decisions is one of the first mental faculties neutralized by alcohol. By removing a person's moral restraints, alcohol becomes a doorway to practically every type of perversion. People say things they wouldn't normally say, they visit places they wouldn't normally visit, and they do things they wouldn't normally do. In his *The Gospel in Leviticus*, J.A. Seiss said:

> "If the effects of alcoholic stimulation went no further than to cloud the mind and stupefy the natural senses of those who indulge in it, it would not be so bad. The great mischief is that, as it clouds the moral nature, it kindles all the bad passions into redoubled activity. It not only enfeebles and expels all impulses of good, but it quickens and enthrones ever latent evil, and fits a man for the ready performance of any vile and sacrilegious deed."[93]

How often have we heard someone comment on the morning after being drunk that they can't believe who they spent the night with or they respond in disbelief when confronted with what they did or said the previous night while drunk? This numbing and dumbing effect of alcohol is undoubtedly the reason the powers of darkness have used it for so many centuries as a primary means of subverting the souls of millions of men and women. No doubt this prompted Solomon to write the following almost 3000 years ago:

"Who has woe? Who has sorrow? Who has strife? Who has complaints? Who has needless bruises? Who has bloodshot eyes? Those who linger over wine, who go to sample bowls of mixed wine. Do not gaze at wine when it is red, when it sparkles in the cup, when it goes down smoothly! In the end it bites like a snake and poisons like a viper. Your eyes will see strange sights and your mind imagine confusing things. You will be like one sleeping on the high seas, lying on top of the rigging. 'They hit me,' you will say, 'but I'm not hurt! They beat me, but I don't feel it! When will I wake up so I can find another drink?'" Proverbs 23:29–35, NIV

OTHER ORGANS AFFECTED BY ALCOHOL

King David, the Old Testament hero said:

"I will praise You, for I am fearfully and wonderfully made;" Psalms 139:14, NKJ

A simple study of human anatomy confirms David's 3000 year old observation. The body is truly a masterpiece of divine workmanship. None of mankind's remarkable inventions or accomplishments has been able to rival the complexity and efficiency of the human body. When creating Adam's body, God combined countless marvels that continue to amaze our greatest scientific minds.

The liver is one of those marvels. According to one nutritional company,

"The liver is one of the most robust organs in the body. It is capable of completely regenerating itself after it has suffered certain types of damage. Up to one quarter of the liver can be removed, and within a short period of time, it will grow back to its original shape and size. But, alcohol is one of the toxins that the liver doesn't handle well and it cannot regenerate itself from the severe damage it causes."[94]

Ultimately, the liver functions as the primary filter for the blood. A healthy liver insures that the blood is cleansed from impurities as it circulates throughout the body. The task of breaking down alcohol and eliminating it from the body is accomplished mainly in the liver. The toxic effect of alcohol on the liver causes excessive amounts of fat to accumulate in the liver reducing its ability to assist in digestion.[95] As these fats are deposited in the liver, it becomes enlarged. Given enough exposure to alcohol, the liver begins to fail. As it fails, it begins to lose the ability to remove yellow pigment from the system causing the skin to turn yellow—a condition known as jaundice. As more damage is done, liver failure causes fluid to build in the extremities—a condition known as edema.

Dr. Michaele Dunlap emphasizes how important the liver is to the body, especially as it assists in eliminating alcohol:

> "Its complex functions are associated with dozens of processes of body chemistry and metabolism. It produces the bile that helps digest fatty foods; it manufactures heparin, an anticoagulant, and it stores and releases sugar. The liver also produces antibodies that help ward off disease, and it cleanses the body of poisons, including alcohol. With small amounts of alcohol, this cleansing can happen effectively. When the amount of alcohol is high, imbalances are created which can lead to hypoglycemia (low blood sugar), hyperuricemia (as in arthritis or gout), fatty liver (which may lead to hepatitis or cirrhosis), and hyperlipemia (build-up of fats sent to the bloodstream; which leads to heart problems)."[96]

Continued, long-term alcohol consumption eventually causes the destruction of liver cells thus covering the liver with irreversible lesions and scars. This condition is known as cirrhosis and is the final stage of liver disease before death. Cirrhosis caused 27,035 American deaths in 2001.[97] Drug Strategies reports that more than 2 million Americans suffer from liver disease caused by heavy drinking.[98]

In addition to the brain and the liver, alcohol also affects other organs and systems in the body. Some of these organs and systems are:

The pancreas—Heavy drinkers have a significant risk of developing pancreatis, a chronic inflammation of the pancreas.

The bones—Alcohol interferes with the body's ability to

absorb calcium causing the bones to become weak, soft, brittle, and thinner—a condition known as osteoporosis.

The stomach & small intestines–Alcohol causes irritation of the stomach lining, peptic ulcers, inflammation, bleeding lesions, and cancer. Alcohol also causes irritation of the lining of the intestinal tract and colon. Chronic drinking may cause ulcers and cancer of the intestines and colon. Alcohol reduces the small intestine's ability to process nutrients and vitamins thus weakening the whole body. Nausea, diarrhea, vomiting, sweating and loss of appetite are common symptoms of heavy drinking.

The reproductive system–Heavy drinking can impair and diminish sexual function causing impotence and infertility. This damage is sometimes permanent. Continued exposure to alcohol increases a female's risk of developing breast cancer. Alcohol consumed during pregnancy increases the risk of birth defects due to Fetal Alcohol Syndrome and Fetal Alcohol Effect.

The throat–Alcohol can irritate and damage the lining of the esophagus, often causing severe vomiting, hemorrhaging, pain, and difficulty in swallowing. Extended, heavy drinking increases the risk of developing throat cancer.

The heart & other muscles–Alcohol reduces the flow of blood to the muscles, including the heart. This reduced blood flow weakens and deteriorates the muscles. In the heart, the outcome is cardiomyopathy—a sluggish heart. Another way that alcohol effects the heart is arrhythmia—an irregular heartbeat, sometimes called "holiday heart" because of the heavy drinking during holiday seasons. All of this results in increased blood pressure and higher risk of heart attack and stroke.

The immunity system–Because heavy drinking has such a damaging effect on the liver and pancreas, the immunity system is weakened, thus reducing the body's ability to fight off disease.[99]

No wonder Abraham Lincoln said, "Alcohol has many defenders but no defense."[100] I couldn't agree more.

Chapter 5

Q UOTES WORTH QUOTING ON ALCOHOL

W hat famous people over the centuries have said about alcohol and its effects is both significant and enlightening to say the least:

"an expression identical with ruin,"[101]
> Laertius Diogenes, referring to drunkenness (Laertius was the Roman writer who lived sometime between 200–300 B.C. and is best known for his biography of the Greek philosophers)

"Drunkenness is nothing but voluntary madness."[102]
> Lucius Annaeus Seneca, the Roman playwright, orator, and philosopher who lived from 4 B.C. to 65 A.D.

"Wine produces mockers; liquor leads to brawls. Whoever is led astray by drink cannot be wise."
> Solomon, Proverbs 20:1, NLT

"My child, listen and be wise. Keep your heart on the right course. Do not carouse with drunkards and gluttons, for they are on their way to poverty."
> Solomon, Proverbs 23:19–21, NLT

"Who has woe? Who has sorrow? Who has strife? Who has complaints? Who has needless bruises? Who has bloodshot eyes? Those who linger over wine, who go to sample bowls of mixed wine. Do not gaze at wine when it is red, when it sparkles in the cup, when it goes down smoothly! In the end it bites like a snake and poisons like a viper. Your eyes will see strange sights and your mind imagine confusing things. You will be like one sleeping on the high seas,

lying on top of the rigging. 'They hit me,' you will say, 'but I'm not hurt! They beat me, but I don't feel it! When will I wake up so I can find another drink?'"
>   Solomon, Proverbs 23:29–35, NIV

"It is not for kings, O Lemuel—not for kings to drink wine, not for rulers to crave beer, lest they drink and forget what the law decrees, and deprive all the oppressed of their rights."
>   Solomon, Proverbs 31:4–5, NIV

"Don't eat meat or drink wine or do anything else if it might cause another Christian to stumble."
>   Paul, the Apostle, Romans 14:21, NLT

"Do not get drunk on wine, which leads to debauchery."
>   Paul, the Apostle, Ephesians 5:18, NIV

"If the ancients drank as our people drink rum and cider, it is no wonder we hear of so many possessed with devils."[103]
>   John Adams, 2nd President of U.S.

"The habit of using ardent spirits by men in public office has often produced more injury to the public service, and more trouble to me, than any other circumstance that has occurred in the internal concerns of the country during my administration. And were I to commence my administration again, with the knowledge which from experience I have acquired, the first question that I would ask with regard to every candidate for office should be, 'Is he addicted to the use of ardent spirits?'"[104]
>   Thomas Jefferson, 3rd President of U.S. & author of the Declaration of Independence

"Nothing has corrupted the legislation of the country more than the use of intoxicating drink."[105]
>   Thomas Jefferson, 3rd President of U.S. & author of the Declaration of Independence

On February 22, 1842, on the occasion of the 110th anniversary of George Washington's birth, Abraham Lincoln gave a speech to the Springfield Washington Temperance Society in Springfield, Illinois. The speech was about the evils of alcohol. The following are excerpts from that speech:

> "Whether or not the world would be vastly benefited by a total and final banishment from it of all intoxicating drinks, seems to me not now an open question. Three-fourths of mankind confess the affirmative with their tongues, and, I believe, all the rest acknowledge it in their hearts."

> "The demon of intemperance ever seems to have delighted in sucking the blood of genius and of generosity. What one of us but can call to mind some dear relative, more promising in youth than all his fellows, who has fallen a sacrifice to his rapacity? He ever seems to have gone forth, like the Egyptian angel of death, commissioned to slay if not the first, the fairest born of every family. Shall he now be arrested in his desolating career? In that arrest, all can give aid that will; and who shall be excused that can, and will not? Far around as human breath has ever blown, he keeps our fathers, our brothers, our sons, and our friends, prostrate in the chains of moral death."

As he continued, Lincoln compared the "temperance revolution" of his day with the American Revolution by saying,

> "Turn now, to the temperance revolution. In it, we shall find a stronger bondage broken; a viler slavery, manumitted; a greater tyrant deposed. In it, more of want supplied, more disease healed, more sorrow assuaged. By it no orphans starving, no widows weeping. By it, none wounded in feeling, none injured in interest . . . And when the victory shall be complete—when there shall be neither a slave nor a drunkard on the earth—how proud the title of the Land, which may truly claim to be the birth-place and the cradle of both those revolutions, that shall have ended in that victory. How nobly distinguished that People, who shall have planted, and nurtured to maturity, both the political and moral freedom of their species."

Lincoln spoke of the relief those who give up liquor feel as they find freedom from its control:

> "But when one, who has long been known as a victim of intemperance bursts the fetters that have bound him, and appears before his neighbors 'clothed, and in his right mind,' a redeemed specimen of long-lost humanity, and stands up with tears of joy trembling in his eyes, to tell of the miseries once endured, now to be endured no more forever; of his once naked and starving children, now clad and fed comfortably; of a wife long weighed down with woe, weeping, and a broken heart, now restored to health, happiness, and a renewed affection; and how easily it is all done, once it is resolved to be done; how simple his language, there is a logic, and an eloquence in it, that few, with human feelings, can resist." [106]

In their book, *Alcohol: The Beloved Enemy,* Dr. Jack Van Impe and Roger Campbell quote Lincoln as having said the following on the day of his death:

> "With the help of the people, we have cleaned up a colossal job. Slavery is abolished. After reconstruction, the next great question will be the abolition of the liquor traffic. My head and heart and my hand and my purse will go into that work. Less than a quarter of a century ago I predicted that the time would come when there would be neither a slave nor a drunkard in the land. I have lived to see, thank God, one of these prophecies fulfilled. I hope to see the other realized." [107]

Billy Sunday was an outspoken opponent of alcohol. The following excerpts are from his famous sermon, "Booze":

> "Whatever takes away the comforts of home, whatever degrades that man or woman, whatever invades the sanctity of the home, is the deadliest foe to the home, to church, to state, and school, and the saloon is the deadliest foe to the home, the church and the state, on top of God Almighty's dirt. And if all the combined forces of hell should assemble in conclave, and with them all the men on earth that hate and despise God, and purity, and virtue, if all the scum of the earth could mingle with the denizens of hell to try to think of the deadliest institution to home, to church, and state, I tell you, sir, the combined hellish intelligence could not conceive of or bring an institution that could touch the hem of the garment of the open licensed saloon to damn the home

and manhood, and womanhood, and business and every other good thing on God's earth."

"The saloon is the sum of all villainies. It is worse than war or pestilence. It is the crime of crimes. It is the parent of crimes and the mother of sins. It is the appalling source of misery and crime in the land. And to license such an incarnate fiend of hell is the dirtiest, low-down, damnable business on top of this old earth. There is nothing to be compared to it."

"Say, if the man that drinks the whisky goes to hell, the man that votes for the saloon that sold the whisky to him will go to hell. If the man that drinks the whisky goes to hell, and the man that sold the whisky to the men that drank it, goes to heaven, then the poor drunkard will have the right to stand on the brink of eternal damnation and put his arms around the pillar of justice, shake his fist in the face of the Almighty and say, 'Unjust! Unjust!' If you vote for the dirty business you ought to go to hell as sure as you live, and I would like to fire the furnace while you are there. Some fellow says, 'Drive the saloon out and the buildings will be empty.' Which would you rather have, empty buildings or empty jails, penitentiaries, and insane asylums? You drink the stuff and what have you to say? You that vote for it and you that sell it? Look at them painted on the canvas of your recollection." [108]

"Out of 21 civilizations preceding this one [America], 19 of them have been destroyed by a mixture of atheism, materialism, and alcoholism."[109]

> Sir Arnold Toynbee, notable historian

"Drunkenness is temporary suicide."[110]

> Bertrand Russell, famous atheist

"As a cure for worry, work is better than whiskey."[111]

> Thomas Edison, scientist & inventor

"To put alcohol in the human brain is like putting sand in the bearings of an engine."[112]

> Thomas Edison, scientist & inventor

"Drink is commercially our greatest wastrel; socially it is our greatest criminal; morally and religiously it is our greatest enemy."[113]
Albert Schweitzer, humanitarian

I find it significant that a Roman philosopher, an ancient king, former Presidents of the U.S., a former professional baseball player and ex-heavy drinker, a noted historian, one of the most celebrated scientists and inventors in history, a famous humanitarian, and a hardened atheist—just to name a few, all agreed that alcohol and the drunkenness it often produces has been one of the greatest scourges our nation, and mankind in general, has ever encountered.

Chapter 6

I N THE BEGINNING . . . ALCOHOL

Although not a hard-and-fast rule, normally, the way a particular subject is dealt with in its earliest biblical references indicates the Bible's overall position on that subject. So as we begin our biblical discussion on alcohol, it is important that we pay close attention to its first few appearances in Scripture.

Of the first three times alcohol is mentioned in the Bible, two are negative—extremely negative. In fact, these early passages are one of the proofs of the Bible's divine origin. The often brutal honesty of the Bible—especially when it comes to the lives of its heroes—points to the Scripture's authenticity. Had men invented the biblical account, they certainly wouldn't have included the embarrassing stories it does; but God, of course, tells the whole, sometimes sordid, story.

The first appearance of alcohol in the Bible occurs in Genesis 9. The story involves Noah and his sons and an event that occurred not long after the flood. The passage states:

> "After the Flood, Noah became a farmer and planted a vineyard. One day he became drunk on some wine he had made and lay naked in his tent. Ham, the father of Canaan, saw that his father was naked and went outside and told his brothers. Shem and Japheth took a robe, held it over their shoulders, walked backward into the tent, and covered their father's naked body. As they did this, they looked the other way so they wouldn't see him naked. When Noah woke up from his drunken stupor, he learned what Ham, his youngest son, had done. Then he cursed the descendants of Canaan, the son of Ham:" Genesis 9:20–25, NLT

Although some scholars argue that Noah may not have completely understood the intoxicating power of alcohol, this argument is of little consequence to our discussion here. Regardless of Noah's knowledge of wine and its effects, the fact remains that he did get drunk and the results were devastating. In his drunken state, Noah lay naked in his tent. When Ham saw his father in this pitiful state, he showed such great disrespect toward him that he received a stern rebuke and judgment from Noah.

Some have questioned why the curse was actually pronounced against Canaan, Ham's son, rather than Ham himself. It appears that the judgment on Ham was so severe that it not only impacted him, but his descendants as well. This is not uncommon in Scripture. Often, the children suffer from the consequences of their parents' or other ancestors' sins. Exodus 20:5 tells us that sometimes a particular sin or judgment can follow a family to the third or fourth generation. A simple study of family histories will verify that this principle continues to work even today. No doubt, this is what occurred in the instance of Ham and his descendants.

Of primary interest to us in this study is the reason for this calamity—alcohol. The very first time alcohol makes an appearance in the Bible it is lowering inhibitions (Noah naked in his tent) and is bringing a curse upon others (Ham and his children)—its track record hasn't improved much over the centuries.

The third time alcohol appears in Scripture, we read of a scandalous episode in the life of a man by the name of Lot, nephew to the great Jewish patriarch, Abraham. We find the story in Genesis 19:

> "Afterward Lot left Zoar because he was afraid of the people there, and he went to live in a cave in the mountains with his two daughters. One day the older daughter said to her sister, 'There isn't a man anywhere in this entire area for us to marry. And our father will soon be too old to have children. Come, let's get him drunk with wine, and then we will sleep with him. That way we will preserve our family line through our father.' So that night they got him drunk, and the older daughter went in and slept with her father. He was unaware of her lying down or getting up again.

The next morning the older daughter said to her younger sister, 'I slept with our father last night. Let's get him drunk with wine again tonight, and you go in and sleep with him. That way our family line will be preserved.' So that night they got him drunk again, and the younger daughter went in and slept with him. As before, he was unaware of her lying down or getting up again. So both of Lot's daughters became pregnant by their father." Genesis 19:30–36, NLT

Most are familiar with the story of Lot and his family, who lived in the sin-infested metropolitan area known as Sodom and Gomorrah. Because he was a believer, an angelic escort was sent to remove Lot and his family before God's judgment fell. Children have listened in awe for years to the story of how, on their way out of Sodom, Lot's wife looked back and was turned into a pillar of salt—leaving only Lot and his two daughters to escape from judgment. Although Lot was successful in getting his daughters out of Sodom, unfortunately, he wasn't as successful in getting Sodom out of his daughters.

Afterwards, still controlled by the twisted, perverted thinking of Sodom, Lot's daughters, unwilling to trust God for their futures, determined that their only hope for children was their father. Refusing to resist the temptation of the alcohol they offered him, Lot got drunk and in his drunken stupor, impregnated his own daughters. Although Lot was a true believer (2 Peter 2:7–9), he became a sad example of what can happen when believers imbibe alcohol.

The Bible records numerous other examples detailing alcohol's wicked work:

- 1 Kings 16: Elah, the king of Israel, got drunk and was murdered by Zimri, the captain of his chariots.
- 1 Kings 20: Benhadad, the king of Syria, got drunk and allowed his army to be destroyed and had to flee for his life.
- Daniel 5: Belshazzar, king of the Chaldeans, got drunk and his kingdom was overrun by the Medes and he was slain—all in the same night.

- 1 Corinthians 11: Some of the believers at Corinth were getting drunk during their observance of the Lord's Supper and many of them became ill and some of them died as a direct result of God's judgment.

Even though these passages do not tell alcohol's complete story, they do set a powerful precedent. In these passages, alcohol definitely lived "down" to Solomon's appraisal which he penned in 1000 B.C.:

> "Who has woe? Who has sorrow? Who has strife? Who has complaints? Who has needless bruises? Who has bloodshot eyes? Those who linger over wine, who go to sample bowls of mixed wine. Do not gaze at wine when it is red, when it sparkles in the cup, when it goes down smoothly! In the end it bites like a snake and poisons like a viper. Your eyes will see strange sights and your mind imagine confusing things." Proverbs 23:29–33, NIV

WHAT'S YOUR INTERPRETATION?

Before we can understand what the Bible says about alcohol (or any other subject), we must be certain that we know how to correctly interpret it. Many wrong beliefs and teachings have resulted from poor interpretation of the Bible. We must keep in mind when reading the Bible, that we cannot arbitrarily determine what "we think" it is saying. Ultimately, like any other work of literature, the Bible is a literal work, says what it means, and should say the same thing to everyone. Certainly a passage may have numerous layers of meaning that can all speak strongly to us at different times, but the message we get from any passage of Scripture must always be consistent with the context of that passage and consistent with the overall message of the Bible. To insure that the Bible (and all other works of literature for that matter) is interpreted correctly and consistently, there are rules of interpretation that we must obey. This collection of rules for interpreting the Bible is called hermeneutics. Scholars have used these rules of hermeneutics for centuries to guarantee that the Bible is interpreted as clearly and correctly as possible.

Though we do not have to be an accomplished student of hermeneutics to understand the Bible, it is imperative that we have at least a cursory understanding of its principles. If we desire to skillfully handle God's Word as 2 Timothy 2:15 commands, the following principles of interpretation are essential:

1. We must remember that the Bible is divinely inspired and, in its original text, is inerrant.

The Bible is not human (men did not invent it), but divine in origin. Therefore, when reading the Bible we must remember that we're reading the inspired (God-breathed) Word of God and should use the utmost care when attempting to interpret it.

> "Above all, you must understand that no prophecy in Scripture ever came from the prophets themselves or because they wanted to prophesy. It was the Holy Spirit who moved the prophets to speak from God." 2 Peter 2:20–21, NLT

> "All Scripture is inspired [God-breathed] by God and is useful to teach us what is true and to make us realize what is wrong in our lives. It straightens us out and teaches us to do what is right." 2 Timothy 3:16, NLT

2. We should interpret the Bible literally.

The Bible, like any other book, should always be interpreted literally unless it is obvious that symbolic language is being used. Scripture should never be allegorized, "spiritualized," or turned into a metaphor to make a point that the passage does not make originally.

3. We need spiritual help in understanding the Bible.

Since the Bible is a supernatural book, only those who have the indwelling Holy Spirit can properly understand its message. The believer must look to the Holy Spirit for illumination and guidance as he/she seeks to find the true meaning of a particular passage. Jesus said that the Holy Spirit would be our teacher and would guide us as we seek the truths revealed in God's Word.

> "But people who aren't Christians can't understand these truths from God's Spirit. It all sounds foolish to them because only those who have the Spirit can understand what the Spirit means." 1 Corinthians 2:14, NLT

> "When the Spirit of truth comes, he will guide you into all truth." John 16:13, NLT

4. We must consider the context of the passage.

A passage should always be interpreted within the context it was written. Also, a general understanding of the author and theme as well as the historical and geographical context of a particular passage is critical to properly understanding its message. It has been said that a text taken out of context for a proof-text (a single passage used to prove a principle that is usually unscriptural) is often nothing more than a pretext.

5. We must read the Bible holistically.

No passage of Scripture should be interpreted independent of the rest of Scripture. No Scripture can be interpreted in such a way that it is contradictory to other Scriptures. In other words, the Bible, correctly understood, does not contradict itself.

6. We must observe the laws of grammar when reading the Bible.

The rules of grammar, both of the original and the receptor language should be observed as the Bible is read. Periods, commas, question marks, paragraph delineations, pronouns, verb tenses, etc. should be carefully observed.

7. We should use the Bible to interpret the Bible.

In the Bible, there are passages that are both easy and difficult to understand. The passages that are more easily understood should be used to assist in interpreting the more difficult ones. In short, we should master the easiest passages first and then use them to shed light on the more difficult passages. If allowed to, the Bible will interpret itself.

There is one other principle I believe we must observe when studying God's Word: we must study the writings of thousands of committed believers who, over the centuries, have spent their lives poring over the oldest biblical manuscripts available. Many of these writers (Hebrew and Greek scholars) have provided valuable works that are essential reading for the serious Bible student. Because of their combined efforts, few, if any, "scriptural rocks" have remained unturned as the Bible has been studied and re-studied thousands and thousands of times. We have the tremendous opportunity to "stand on their shoulders" by taking advantage of their study as we seek to correctly understand the message of Scripture.

As we observe these principles of interpretation, we can be assured that we are discovering the exact meaning the author intended. As we do, we guard ourselves against the extreme, personal, and often unbiblical interpretations that confuse and mislead many.

GOOD AND BAD WINE

Depending on the version of the Bible used, the word 'wine' appears some 237 times. Of those numerous references, it is viewed in two basic ways: as a blessing and as a curse. How can it be that the Bible has two, such contradictory positions on the same subject? Some insist it doesn't and that the wines of the Bible were always fermented. But if they were, how could God call something that causes such carnage a blessing? This begs the question, "Are the wines of the Bible always the fermented type?" It seems that the only way something as powerful as wine can be both a blessing and a curse is if two different kinds of wines are being discussed—fermented and unfermented. Consider these examples:

Wine = a blessing:
- "Then Melchizedek, the king of Salem and a priest of God Most High, brought him [Abraham] bread and wine." Genesis 14:18, NLT
- "May God always give you plenty of dew for healthy crops and good harvests of grain and wine." Genesis 27:28, NLT
- "It will be an offering given to the LORD by fire, and it will be very pleasing to him. Along with this sacrifice, you must also offer one quart of wine as a drink offering." Leviticus 23:13, NLT
- " . . . then he will send the rains in their proper seasons so you can harvest crops of grain, grapes for wine, and olives for oil." Deuteronomy 11:14, NLT
- "But the grapevine replied, 'should I quit producing the wine that cheers both God and people, just to wave back and forth over the trees?'" Judges 9:13, NLT
- "You allow them to produce food from the earth—wine to make them glad," Psalms 104:14–15, NLT
- "Honor the LORD with your wealth and with the best part of everything your land produces. Then he will fill your barns with grain, and your vats will overflow with the finest wine." Proverbs 3:9–10, NLT
- "Is anyone thirsty? Come and drink—even if you have no money! Come, take your choice of wine or milk—it's all free!" Isaiah 55:1, NLT
- "Then the LORD will pity his people and be indignant for the honor of his land! He will reply, 'Look! I am sending you grain and wine and olive oil, enough to satisfy your needs.'" Joel 2:18–19, NLT
- "In that day the mountains will drip with sweet wine, and the hills will flow with milk." Joel 3:18, NLT
- "He went to him and bandaged his wounds, pouring on oil and wine." Luke 10:34, NIV
- "'Usually a host serves the best wine first,' he said. 'Then, when everyone is full and doesn't care, he brings out the less expen-

sive wines. But you have kept the best until now!'" John 2:10, NLT

- "Don't drink only water. You ought to drink a little wine for the sake of your stomach because you are sick so often." 1 Timothy 5:23, NLT

Wine = a curse:
- "One day he [Noah] became drunk on some wine he had made and lay naked in his tent." Genesis 9:21, NLT
- "Come, let's get him [Lot] drunk with wine, and then we will sleep with him. That way we will preserve our family line through our father." Genesis 19:32, NLT
- "Then the LORD said to Aaron, 'You and your descendants must never drink wine or any other alcoholic drink before going into the Tabernacle. If you do, you will die. This is a permanent law for you, and it must be kept by all future generations.'" Leviticus 10:8–9, NLT
- "If some of the people, either men or women, take the special vow of a Nazirite, setting themselves apart to the LORD in a special way, they must give up wine and other alcoholic drinks. They must not use vinegar made from wine, they must not drink other fermented drinks or fresh grape juice, and they must not eat grapes or raisins. As long as they are bound by their Nazirite vow, they are not allowed to eat or drink anything that comes from a grapevine, not even the grape seeds or skins." Numbers 6:2–4, NLT
- "The angel of the LORD appeared to Manoah's wife and said, 'Even though you have been unable to have children, you will soon become pregnant and give birth to a son [Samson]. You must not drink wine or any other alcoholic drink or eat any forbidden food.'" Judges 13:3–4, NLT
- "They eat the bread of wickedness and drink the wine of violence." Proverbs 4:17, NIV
- "Wine produces mockers; liquor leads to brawls. Whoever is led astray by drink cannot be wise." Proverbs 20:1, NLT

- "Do not carouse with drunkards and gluttons, for they are on their way to poverty." Proverbs 23:20–21, NLT
- "Who has woe? Who has sorrow? Who has strife? Who has complaints? Who has needless bruises? Who has bloodshot eyes? Those who linger over wine, who go to sample bowls of mixed wine. Do not gaze at wine when it is red, when it sparkles in the cup, when it goes down smoothly! In the end it bites like a snake and poisons like a viper. Your eyes will see strange sights and your mind imagine confusing things. You will be like one sleeping on the high seas, lying on top of the rigging. 'They hit me,' you will say, 'but I'm not hurt! They beat me, but I don't feel it! When will I wake up so I can find another drink?'" Proverbs 23:29–35, NIV
- "It is not for kings, O Lemuel—not for kings to drink wine, not for rulers to crave beer, lest they drink and forget what the law decrees, and deprive all the oppressed of their rights." Proverbs 31:4–5, NIV
- "Woe to those who rise early in the morning to run after their drinks, who stay up late at night till they are inflamed with wine." Isaiah 5:11, NIV
- "Destruction is certain for those who are heroes when it comes to drinking, who boast about all the liquor they can hold." Isaiah 5:22, NLT
- "Now, however, Israel is being led by drunks! The priests and prophets reel and stagger from beer and wine. They make stupid mistakes as they carry out their responsibilities." Isaiah 28:7, NLT
- "The priests must never drink wine before entering the inner courtyard." Ezekiel 44:21, NLT
- "But Daniel made up his mind not to defile himself by eating the food and wine given to them by the king." Daniel 1:8, NLT
- "As they drank the wine, they praised the gods of gold and silver, of bronze, iron, wood and stone." Daniel 5:4, NIV

- "Alcohol and prostitution have robbed my people of their brains." Hosea 4:11, NLT
- "Don't eat meat or drink wine or do anything else if it might cause another Christian to stumble." Romans 14:21, NLT
- "Do not get drunk on wine, which leads to debauchery." Ephesians 5:18, NIV
- "[a pastor should be one] not given to drunkenness . . ." 1 Timothy 3:3, NIV
- "Deacons, likewise, are to be men worthy of respect, sincere, not indulging in much wine . . ." 1 Timothy 3:8, NIV
- "For you have spent enough time in the past doing what pagans choose to do—living in debauchery, lust, drunkenness, orgies, carousing and detestable idolatry." 1 Peter 4:3, NIV

How can the Bible say in Judges 9:13 that wine is good, in Proverbs 3:9–10 call it God's blessing to those who honor Him, and yet, forbid the priests to drink it in Leviticus 10:8–9, warn us in Proverbs 20:1 that it is a mocker, and forbid us to even look at it (much less drink it) in Proverbs 23:29–35? The only way it can consistently do this is if it is talking about two different kinds of wines. So, how do we determine which type of wine is being discussed in a particular passage? By understanding two things: the original word translated as "wine" and the context in which the word "wine" is used.

Before exploring the original words translated as "wine" in our English Bibles, one more important question must be answered: What were the wines of Bible times like and how did the people use them? The facts may surprise us.

Chapter 7

Wines in Bible Times

A book of this type would be incomplete if it did not contain enough historical and technical data to prove its premise. Therefore, this chapter will cover much of what we know about the history of the wines used in the times the Bible was written. I have attempted to make this part of our study flow as smoothly as possible, but admittedly, some of the material in this chapter is challenging. I encourage you to hang in there, read this information carefully, and trust that when you finish, you'll be prepared to run the final leg of this journey with me. So buckle up, because here she goes . . .

When studying about the wines of the Bible, one of the most common mistakes made is assuming that most of those who lived in Bible times habitually drank fermented, intoxicating wines. Over the years when discussing this subject with others, I have discovered that some seem to believe that many of the saints, both in the Old and New Testaments, were literally drunks because the Bible says they drank so much wine (the assumption is made that all wines in the Bible were fermented). After visiting with these people, I have often asked myself, "How in the world did they come to this conclusion?" The only answers I can imagine are:

1. They simply do not understand what the Bible is communicating when it speaks of wine.
2. They are ignorant of history.
3. They approach the subject with a bias in favor of believers drinking alcohol.

OLD TESTAMENT SAINTS OR DRUNKS?

A good place to begin this discussion is to understand that it was primarily the barbarians, not the believers, who made the drinking of intoxicating beverages and drunkenness a common practice in ancient times. Consider this quote:

> "Drinking unmixed wine was looked upon by the Greek culture as barbaric. Professor Robert Stein in his 'Wine-drinking in New Testament Times' (*Christianity* Today, June 20, 1975: 9–11), quotes Mnesitheus of Athens as saying, 'The gods have revealed wine to mortals, to be the greatest blessing for those who use it aright, but for those who use it without measure, the reverse. For it gives food to them that take it and strength in mind and body. In medicine it is most beneficial; it can be mixed with liquid and drugs and it brings aid to the wounded. In daily intercourse, to those who mix and drink it moderately, it gives good cheer; but if you overstep the bounds, it brings violence. Mix it half and half, and you get madness; unmixed, bodily collapse.'[114]

This is confirmed by the Apostle Peter:

> "For you have spent enough time in the past doing what **pagans** choose to do—living in debauchery, lust, **drunkenness**, orgies, carousing and detestable idolatry." 1 Peter 4:3, NIV

Many of the historians and philosophers of antiquity spoke about two types of wine: sweet, unfermented, un-intoxicating wine and the wine that most of us are familiar with that was fermented and would intoxicate. These writers provide a window that allows us to see into their world. From the book, *Bible Wines,* we learn that the ancients *preferred* the unfermented, un-intoxicating wines (often boiled or filtered to keep them from fermenting) over the fermented ones:

1. **Aristotle**: This Greek philosopher spoke of sweet wine as a wine that would not intoxicate. He said that the wine of Arcadia was so thick that it was necessary to scrape it from the skin bottles in which it was contained, and dissolve the scrapings in water.

2. **Virgil**: This Latin writer born in 70 B.C. said that boiling wine was the best way to make it good.

3. **Homer**: He wrote in the *Odyssey*, book 9, that Ulysses drank a wine that was sweet as honey—imperishable and able to be kept forever; and that when it was drunk, it was diluted with twenty parts water, producing a sweet and divine odor.

4. **Plutarch**: Born in 60 A.D., this Greek philosopher wrote in his *Symposium* that wine is rendered feeble in strength when it is frequently filtered. With its strength thus weakened, the wine would neither inflame the brain nor infest the mind and the passions, and made it much more pleasant to drink.

5. **Horace**: The Latin poet born in 65 B.C. wrote that no wine was sweeter to drink than that which had been boiled. He said it was like nectar and resembled ambrosia more than wine and was perfectly harmless and would not produce intoxication. He said that by also filtering their wines, the ancients rendered them more liquid, weaker, lighter, sweeter, and more pleasant to drink. He encouraged the people of his day to drink cups of this un-intoxicating wine. Knowing how damaging fermented wines were, he discouraged the competitors in the Olympic Games from drinking them.

6. **Columella**: A Latin writer who lived in the time of the Apostles encouraged the use of un-intoxicating wines. He wrote that in Italy and Greece it was common to boil wines to keep them from fermenting. He encouraged taking fresh wines and filtering them in order to make them "sweet, durable, and healthy to the body." In describing this unfermented wine, he wrote that it was good wine and harmless because it "would not affect the nerves," but at the same time, was not deficient in flavor. He suggested that these new wines should be stored in new containers.

7. **Pliny the Elder**: The Roman historian wrote, "The most useful wine has all its force or strength broken by the filter." He wrote that some Roman wines were as thick as honey. He wrote that Albanian wines were sweet and luscious and that some Spanish

wines were un-intoxicating, calling them 'sober wines.' He also wrote that many of the intoxicating wines of his day produced headaches, dropsy, madness, and stomach problems.

8. **Archbishop Potter**: Born in 1674, he wrote in his *Grecian Antiquities* that the ancients "used to boil their wines upon the fire till the fifth part was consumed; then after four years were expired, began to drink them." He went on to quote the celebrated mid-fourth century B.C. philosopher Democritus who traveled over the greater part of Europe, Asia, and Africa, and said that the ancients referred to boiled juice as wine. He also quoted Palladius, the Greek physician as making the same statements.

9. **W.G. Brown**: Having traveled extensively in Africa, Egypt, and Syria from 1792–1798 A.D., Brown wrote that "the wines of Syria are most of them prepared by boiling immediately after they are expressed from the grape, till they are considerably reduced in quantity, when they were put into jars or large bottles and preserved for use." He added, "There is reason to believe that this mode of boiling was a general practice among the ancients."

10. **Caspar Neuman, M.D.**: He was Professor of Chemistry in Berlin in 1795 and wrote, "It is observable that when sweet juices are boiled down to a thick consistence, they not only do not ferment in that state, but are not easily brought into fermentation when diluted with as much water as they had lost in evaporation."

11. **Dr. A. Russell**: In his *Natural History of Aleppo,* he wrote that the wines of Helbon that were in great use among the people had the appearance of coarse honey and were sweet because fermentation had been prevented from occurring.[115]

All of the evidence is quite convincing and gives ample proof that the ancients did not drink intoxicating wines only. Even though intoxicating wines were certainly made and consumed by many in Bible times, the ancients frowned upon drunkenness then, as many of us do today.

IF YOU'VE SIPPED ONE WINE, YOU'VE SIPPED 'EM ALL?

In addition to the misconception that those in ancient times *preferred* fermented wines to unfermented wines is the mistaken notion that wines in the Bible were *always* fermented. This is simply not the case. Just because the Bible speaks of fermented wine in one passage does not mean that it is speaking of fermented wine in *every* passage. But ironically, this is not the common view; many believe that since *some* wines referred to in the Bible are fermented, all are. Frankly, this type of reasoning isn't even logical. Consider this quote from William Patton:

> "[In the Bible] We find the word which denotes the spirit often rendered wind or breath; shall we, therefore, conclude it always means wind or breath, and, with the Sadducees, infer that there is neither angel nor spirit, and that there can be no resurrection? So, also, because the word translated heaven often means the atmosphere, shall we conclude that it always means atmosphere, and that there is no such place as a heaven where the redeemed will be gathered and where is the throne of God?

> But the misery and delusion are that most readers of the Bible, knowing of no other than the present wines of commerce, which are intoxicating, leap to the conclusion, wine is wine all the world over—as the wine of our day is inebriating, therefore the wine mentioned in the Bible was intoxicating, and there was none other.

> There is a perverse tendency in the human mind to limit a generic word to a particular species."[116]

Commenting on this tendency, John Stuart Mill, in his book, *System of Logic,* said:

> "A generic term is always liable to become limited to a single species if people have occasion to think and speak of that species more often

than of anything else contained in the genus. The tide of custom first drifts the word on the shore of a particular meaning, then retires and leaves it there."[117]

Although it may seem quite natural for the reader to associate wines in Scripture (fermented & unfermented) with today's wines (which are all fermented), this assumption is incorrect and leads to a great deal of confusion on the subject. Even though the ancients did make fermented wines, their wines were much weaker than the wines of today. The distillation process used in making today's very strong alcoholic beverages was not even discovered until the 9th century and was utterly unknown to the Hebrews and indeed, to the whole world in ancient times.[118] *Therefore, the ancients didn't even have the ability to make liquors with the strength of those we make today.* To understand how Bible wines compare with those of today, consider this quote:

> "According to the Alcohol Council, beer has approximately 4% alcohol, wine 9–11% alcohol, brandy 15–20% alcohol, and hard liquor 40–50% alcohol (80–100 proof). Wine in biblical times measured at approximately 9–11% alcohol and anyone who drank 15–50% alcohol in those days would have definitely been considered a barbarian. The weakest kind of mixed wine was mixed at a 3:1 ratio and would therefore have been between 2.25–2.75% alcohol. By today's standards, a drink has to exceed 3.2% to be considered an alcoholic beverage. The wine they consumed was either completely non-alcoholic or sub-alcoholic by today's standards. To become drunk with wine in those days you would have to drink all day. That is why the Bible commands elders in the church, 'do not linger long beside your wine' (1 Tim.3:3). With such a low alcoholic content, you would have to purpose to become drunk."[119]

Numerous sources prove that the ancients of Bible times made a distinction between new wine and intoxicating wine. New or sweet wine was the sweet juice extracted from the grape before it could ferment. Professor Moses Stuart said:

> "Facts show that the ancients not only preserved their wine unfer-

mented, but regarded it as of a higher flavor and finer quality than fermented wine."[120]

The difficulty they faced was preserving those juices in their sweet, unfermented state.

Since grapes were a major crop in the lands of the Bible, grape juice (wine) was one of the popular drinks of that area. Rev. Henry Homes, missionary to Constantinople, said:

> "The fabricating of intoxicating liquor was never the chief object for which the grape was cultivated among the Jews. Joined with bread, fruits, and the olive-tree, the three might well be representatives of the productions most essential to them, at the same time they most abundantly provided for the support of life . . . of the sixteen uses of the grape, wine-making was the least important."[121]

We must try to understand how important it was to the ancients to keep their juices from fermenting. Consider the impact to their society if most or all of their juices (wines) had been fermented. Drunkenness would have been epidemic and runaway alcoholism would have, for the most part, rendered life unproductive and almost meaningless. This is exactly why they resorted to such drastic measures to insure that most of their juices did not ferment.

THE PROCESS OF FERMENTATION

At this point, a basic discussion of the process of fermentation would probably be helpful. Once again, it is important for us to remember that the word "wine" in the Bible refers not only to fermented drinks, but to natural, unfermented juices as well. As we have already seen, those living in Bible times knew nothing of distillation, and therefore they were incapable of making alcoholic beverages as strong as ours are today; even their strong alcoholic drinks were weak by today's standards.

One common fallacy concerning wine-making is that juices, if allowed to (even if by accident) will naturally ferment into a desirable alcoholic drink. This simply is not the case. Fermented wines with desirable taste do not occur naturally but instead are man-made. The 19th century eminent French chemist, Jean-Antoine Chaptal, wrote, "Nature never forms spirituous liquors; she rots the grape upon the branch; but it is art which converts the juice into (alcoholic) wine."[122] The Italian writer, Adam Fabroni declared, "Grape-juice does not ferment in the grape itself."[123] The Bible actually acknowledges that it is new wine which is found in the grape: "Thus says the Lord: 'As the new wine is found in the cluster,'" Isaiah 65:8, NKJV. In *The Bible and Its Wines,* Charles W. Ewing wrote:

> "Fermented wine is not the product of the vine. Chemically it is entirely different from the sweet and unfermented grape juice. Fermented wine is 14% alcohol, and it has other constituents that are not found in the fresh grape juice. Alcohol does not grow on the vine. It is not a vine product. Alcohol is the product of decay, the product of fermentation. It is produced by the process of spoiling."[124]

Since fermentation is actually a process of deterioration or decay, it must be carefully monitored and controlled if desirable tasting wines are to be its product. Using fermentation to produce wine is, in fact, a very complicated process. In his article, "The Fungus among Us: A Primer on Yeast," John MacDougall points out the complexity of wine fermentation:

> "However, if you think fermentation is a plain and simple process, you've got another thing coming. Did you know that it is possible to earn a Ph.D. degree in fermentation science? Fermentation is a very, very complex process. Let's try to get at the basics and move up from there. The dictionary describes fermentation as *'Any group of chemical reactions induced by living or non-living ferments that split complex organic compounds into relatively simple substances, esp. the anaerobic conversion of sugar to carbon dioxide and alcohol by yeast.'* Seems plain and simple, doesn't it? Well it is not. After you pitch [add] your yeast, there are thousands of chemical reactions occurring to convert sugar into carbon dioxide and alcohol. There are also a couple of growth phases that the yeast undergoes in order to get to the stage of fermen-

tation. Each of these growth phases is characterized by its own set of chemical reactions depending upon the needs of the yeast."[125]

When grapes are harvested from the vine, they are naturally covered with particles of yeast, mold, and bacteria. When the juice is extracted, if these "natural contaminants" are not removed, in a short period of time, the juice will begin to naturally ferment (decay) into an acidic, vinegar-like wine (sour wine) which is undesirable for drinking. These contaminants can be eliminated from the grapes before the juice is extracted using sulfur dioxide which functions as a disinfectant. After this process is completed, the juice will not ferment and can be preserved for long periods of time as a sweet, un-intoxicating wine.

One of the oldest ways to ferment juice is to allow it to ferment naturally in sealed wooden barrels. These barrels must be stored in a cool place and in a period of a few weeks to a few months the juice will ferment into alcoholic wine. But, the most common way wines are made involves the removal of the "natural contaminants" and the addition of yeast to initiate fermentation. More than just an ingredient, yeast is a single-celled organism that converts the sugar in the juice into carbon dioxide and alcohol. As the carbon dioxide and alcohol are being formed, the temperature of the juice begins to increase. This increase in temperature is problematic since yeast can only survive within a specific range of temperatures. To compensate for this, winemakers cool the fermentation containers to keep the wine from getting too hot. (Too high of a temperature will kill the yeast and stop fermentation.) But temperature is not the only thing the winemaker must control; he must be mindful of numerous other factors as well. Here are a few of the conditions that must be satisfied for successful wine fermentation:

- The temperature of the juice must be kept within certain tolerances or the yeast will die and fermentation will cease.

- Any sudden, extreme change in temperature will kill the yeast and stop fermentation.
- Oxygen must be absent or oxidation will occur and encourage the growth of vinegar-forming bacteria in the juice.
- The juice must be of a certain consistency because too much sugar or too much water will prevent proper fermentation.
- The quantity of yeast must be well regulated, too much or not enough will impede fermentation.

As fermentation continues, pieces of grape skins and pulp begin to rise to the surface. As they accumulate on the surface, they form a filmy "cap" and if allowed to, will dry, forming a seal over the whole mixture. If this cap is allowed to remain, it will decay and become the breeding ground for harmful bacteria ruining the wine. Because this cap seals the fermenting juice, it also holds in the heat which will eventually kill the yeast and stop fermentation. To prevent this, the winemaker must stir the wine (usually twice a day) to force this cap back into the fermenting mixture. Eventually (in anywhere from 4–30 days), the alcohol content will reach 14–15%, the yeast will die, and the fermentation process will stop. Left behind in the wine will be the dead yeast cells (called lees) and other particles which must be removed in a process called "racking." Some wines remain cloudy from these suspended particles for long periods of time and must be eventually filtered or purified by any number of processes. Usually an antiseptic agent is then added to the wine to prevent future microbe development. After this, the wine is ready for consumption or aging.

From this it is easy to see that making good-tasting, fermented wine is no accidental, haphazard process. This is why it is so incorrect to assume that the juices of the ancients fermented into preferable alcoholic wines by accident or simple neglect. It is true that juices can naturally ferment but the end product is a sour wine that tastes like vinegar. The production of drinkable, good-tasting, fermented wine is a detailed and lengthy process and is as much an art as it is a science—hardly the result of luck, chance, or neglect.

Also worth noting is the fact that the hot, dry climate of the lands of the Bible provided a real challenge to the ancients when it came to preserving their juices. The high temperatures made it difficult for them to keep their wines from naturally fermenting into sour wines (vinegar). This is why they had to resort to a number of measures to keep fermentation from occurring. For instance, they often boiled their grape juice—a process that killed the yeast thereby preserving their juice in its sweet, unfermented state for long periods of time. They also sometimes filtered the yeast out of the juice to keep it from fermenting. In the insightful book, *Bible Wines,* we find this helpful information:

> "The ancients had a motive for boiling the unfermented juice. They knew from experience that the juice, by reason of the heat of the climate and the sweetness of the grapes, would speedily turn sour. To preserve it sweet, they naturally resorted to the simple and easy method of boiling."[126]

To keep their wines (juices) from fermenting, the ancients, who preferred the taste of sweet wine over that which was fermented, used the following techniques:

1. They sealed the juice in air-tight containers [new wineskins].
2. They boiled down the juice; turning it into a thick, sweet syrup that wouldn't ferment.
3. They filtered the juice, a process that removed the yeast.
4. They often used sulfur in their juices which prevented fermentation.
5. They lowered the temperature of the wine to 45 degrees and removed the clear liquid which stopped the process of fermentation.[127]

The following story documented by Professor M. Stuart

in 1848 further illustrates the fact that popular wines around the world have often been unfermented:

> "In the early 1800's, the Honorable O. Elsworth, the Chief-Justice of the U.S. Supreme Court, was on his way to France as ambassador, accompanied by Judge Swift, of Connecticut, as secretary, when they were ship-wrecked and cast upon the coast of Spain. On their way to Paris, among the mountains of Spain, a wine was strongly urged upon them which would not intoxicate. Judge Swift first made the experiment on himself. He found that it did not produce any tendency of the kind. The Chief-Justice and [Judge Swift] used to drink a bottle each with their dinner, and a small bottle at night. It was found to be a precious balm to the ambassador, who had become fearfully exhausted by continued sea-sickness . . . Judge Swift assured me that he never, before or since, tasted of anything that would bear comparison with the delicacy and exquisite flavor and refreshing effect of this wine, when taken with due preparation of cooling and mixing with water. He expressed his confident belief that a gallon of it drunk at a time, if a man could swallow down so much, would not affect his head in the least degree."

I believe all of this information sufficiently proves that not all of the wines of the ancients were fermented. Consequently, every time we encounter the word "wine" in the Bible, we shouldn't automatically jump to the conclusion that it means fermented wine. This will have an enormous impact on the way we read and interpret Scripture.

IT'S ALL GREEK AND HEBREW TO ME

The original manuscripts of the Bible were written in Hebrew (Old Testament) and Greek (New Testament). Since most of us do not speak/read the Hebrew or Greek language, it's all pretty much "Greek" to us. So, do we have to be Hebrew/Greek scholars to understand the Bible? No. But even though we don't have to know Hebrew and Greek to understand the message of Scripture, a basic understanding of the original languages helps to shed additional light on many passages. Thankfully, there are numerous commentaries (some written by Hebrew and Greek scholars) to assist us in this task.

From these scholars' works, we find that the following six words (3 Greek and their Hebrew counterparts) are the ones most often translated "wine" in the Bible:

1. **Oinos** (Grk)/**Yayin** (Heb):

The most common word used in the New Testament for wine is the Greek word *oinos*. Its counterpart in the Old Testament is the word *Yayin* that comes from the root word which means to "bubble up" or "boil up." These are general words that refer to the juice of the grape and can refer to both fermented and unfermented wine. Their specific meanings must often be determined by the context in which they are used. "The 1901 Jewish Encyclopedia (vol. 12, p. 533) states that *Yayin,* at least in the rabbinic period, was normally diluted with water to reduce its strength. According to Professor Samuel Lee of Cambridge University, 'Yayin does not refer only to intoxicating liquor made by fermentation, but more often refers to a thick, un-intoxicating syrup or jam, produced by boiling to make it storable.'"[128]

2. **Gleukos** (Grk)/**Tirosh** (Heb):

The Greek word *gleukos* and the Hebrew word *Tirosh* both refer to new, unfermented wine. This type of wine was made from grape juice that was comparatively fresh and had not normally been given the time to ferment. *Gleukos* is the word from which we derive the English word *glucose* which refers to sugar. Quite often, the grape juice was boiled to remove most of the liquid, creating a thick, sweet syrup called *gleukos* that would not ferment. This substance was often spread on bread and eaten much like our jams today. This "jam" was also mixed with water and consumed as a sweet drink that was extremely popular among the ancients.

3. **Sikera** (Grk)/**Shakar** (Heb):

The New Testament word *sikera* and the Old Testament

word *shakar* are the words commonly used for strong, fermented wine. These words are sometimes used generically in the Bible and can refer to both fermented and unfermented wines; therefore the context in which they are used determines what kind of wine is being discussed. Professor M. Stuart said, "The true, original idea of *shakar* is a liquor obtained from dates or other fruits (grapes excepted), or barley, millet, etc., which were dried, or scorched and a decoction of them was mixed with honey, aromatics, etc."[129] "According to the 1901 Jewish Encyclopedia, *shakar* refers to unmixed [full strength], wine."[130]

A good understanding of the words translated "wine" in the Bible provides further evidence that not all of the wines mentioned in Scripture are fermented. The general rule is: if the biblical context speaks positively, it is referring to unfermented wine and if it speaks negatively, it is speaking of fermented wine. Here are some examples:

Positive (unfermented):
- "May God always give you plenty of dew for healthy crops and good harvests of grain and wine [*tirosh*]." Genesis 27:28, NLT
- " . . . then he will send the rains in their proper seasons so you can harvest crops of grain, grapes for wine [*tirosh*], and olives for oil." Deuteronomy 11:14, NLT
- "Honor the LORD with your wealth and with the best part of everything your land produces. Then he will fill your barns with grain, and your vats will overflow with the finest wine [*tirosh*]." Proverbs 3:9–10, NLT
- "Then the LORD will pity his people and be indignant for the honor of his land! He will reply, 'Look! I am sending you grain and wine [*tirosh*] and olive oil, enough to satisfy your needs.'" Joel 2:18–19, NLT
- "Don't drink only water. You ought to drink a little wine [*oinos*] for the sake of your stomach because you are sick so often." 1 Timothy 5:23, NLT

Negative (fermented):

- "Wine [*yayin*] produces mockers; liquor [*shakar*] leads to brawls. Whoever is led astray by drink [*shakar*] cannot be wise." Proverbs 20:1, NLT
- "Who has woe? Who has sorrow? Who has strife? Who has complaints? Who has needless bruises? Who has bloodshot eyes? Those who linger over wine [*yayin*], who go to sample bowls of mixed wine [*yayin*]. Do not gaze at wine [*yayin*] when it is red, when it sparkles in the cup, when it goes down smoothly! In the end it bites like a snake and poisons like a viper. Your eyes will see strange sights and your mind imagine confusing things. You will be like one sleeping on the high seas, lying on top of the rigging. 'They hit me,' you will say, 'but I'm not hurt! They beat me, but I don't feel it! When will I wake up so I can find another drink?'" Proverbs 23:29–35, NIV
- "It is not for kings, O Lemuel—not for kings to drink wine [*yayin*], not for rulers to crave beer [*yayin*], lest they drink and forget what the law decrees, and deprive all the oppressed of their rights." Proverbs 31:4–5, NIV
- "Woe to those who rise early in the morning to run after their drinks [*yayin*], who stay up late at night till they are inflamed with wine [*yayin*]." Isaiah 5:11, NIV
- "The priests must never drink wine [*yayin*] before entering the inner courtyard." Ezekiel 44:21, NLT
- "Don't eat meat or drink wine [*oinos*] or do anything else if it might cause another Christian to stumble." Romans 14:21, NLT
- "Do not get drunk on wine [*oinos*], which leads to debauchery." Ephesians 5:18, NIV

To illustrate how the context is often the best, and sometimes only, way to determine what type of wine is being referred to, let's examine a familiar Old Testament passage:

"Come, all you who are thirsty, come to the waters; and you who have no money, come, buy and eat! Come, buy wine and milk without money and without cost." Isaiah 55:1, NIV

In this passage, God is inviting all to come and receive the blessings of salvation (symbolized by wine and milk). Scripture emphasizes that salvation is free and cannot be earned or deserved, so naturally in this passage these blessings are offered free of charge. Since the wine in this passage is compared to milk which we know is harmless, the wine must be equally as harmless—making unfermented wine the only option. God would never use as a symbol of His salvation, something like fermented wine that can cause such damage.

The following quote from William Patton illustrates how relatively easy it is to know which kind of wine a particular passage of Scripture is referring to:

> "In all the passages where good wine is named, there is no lisp of warning, no intimations of danger, no hint of disapprobation, but always of decided approval. How bold and strongly marked is the contrast:
>
> • The *one* the cause of intoxication, of violence, and of woes; the *other* the occasion of comfort and of peace.
>
> • The *one* the cause of irreligion and of self-destruction; the *other* the devout offering of piety on the altar of God.
>
> • The *one* the symbol of the divine wrath; the *other* the symbol of spiritual blessings.
>
> • The *one* the emblem of eternal damnation; the *other* the emblem of eternal salvation"[131]

But someone may ask, "Doesn't the Bible say in Psalms 104:15 and Ecclesiastes 9:7 that fermented wine makes a person happy? So how could drinking it be wrong?"

> "He makes grass grow for the cattle, and plants for man to cultivate—

bringing forth food from the earth: wine that **gladdens the heart of man**, oil to make his face shine, and bread that sustains his heart." Psalms 104:14–15, NIV

"Go, eat your food with gladness, and **drink your wine with a joyful heart**, for it is now that God favors what you do." Ecclesiastes 9:7, NIV

In *What the Bible Teaches about Alcoholic Drink,* Ed Rickard, Ph.D., gives an excellent answer to this question:

"Neither the gladdened heart of Psalm 104:15 nor the merry heart of Ecclesiastes 9:7 alludes to intoxication. In the latter text, drinking wine with a merry heart is parallel to eating bread with joy. The idea is that God intends us to enjoy the nourishment He provides. In the former text, the effect of wine upon the heart is conceived as a real benefit, comparable to the inner strength derived from bread. Therefore, what the text means by gladness cannot be the unwholesome giddiness and detachment caused by an intoxicant, but the soul refreshment afforded by a cool, sweet beverage. It is a sign of our roots in a corrupt culture that we should, in our interpretation of this text, imagine that gladdening of the heart is a specific benefit of alcoholic wine. Alcoholic wine is an acquired taste, relished only by those who learn to discount the tartness and to tolerate the alcohol. The taste of grape juice brings gladness and pleasure to every drinker."[132]

PROHIBITION

With the passing of the Volsted Act, the 18th Amendment to the U.S. Constitution, alcohol was illegal in the U.S from January 17, 1920 until December 6, 1933. But, did prohibition work? In their book, *Alcohol: The Beloved Enemy,* Dr. Jack Van Impe and Roger Campbell give a convincing argument that it actually did work and that it had a very positive effect on the moral and physical health of our nation.[133] It is unfortunate that some of the criminals of that era like the infamous Chicagoan, Al Capone, grabbed all of the headlines making it appear as though what was going on in cites like Chicago was going on all over the nation. Although liquor was available to those willing to break the law to get it, it appears that prohibition greatly reduced the use, abuse, and devastating effects of alcohol. This was confirmed by William Plymat, when he was the executive director of the American Council on Alcohol Problems:

> "During the period when national prohibition was in effect in the United States, consumption of alcohol was low and there were relatively few alcohol problems, and the cost to society of these problems was very little. Then as legal alcoholic beverages came into being, the first results noticed by society seemed to be the tax revenues received by federal and state governments. This was what might be thought of as a 'first' effect of legal alcohol.

> As the years rolled by, the consumption of alcohol constantly increased. It was a gradually escalating condition, and in recent years the escalation has speeded up until today we are facing a monstrous problem. As a society, are we close to hitting bottom?"[134]

Whether or not you and I agree that our nation would be better off if alcohol were once again made illegal, one thing is certain—the Bible clearly places it on the "top ten most wanted" list. As we begin to piece together the facts concerning fermented wine, it is easy to see why God prohibited many in Old Testament times from using it. Here are some of those prohibitions:

• The priests were prohibited from drinking alcohol.

> "Then the Lord said to Aaron, you and your descendants must never drink wine or any other alcoholic drink before going into the Tabernacle. If you do, you will die. This is a permanent law for you, and it must be kept by all future generations." Leviticus 10:8–9, NLT

Even though some believe this prohibition only applied to the priests when serving in the temple, I am convinced that God intended the priests to practice total abstinence. There are numerous reasons why I believe this. In the first place, the priests were to be spiritual examples to all of God's people. Like spiritual leaders in the New Testament era, the priests were to live lives that were beyond reproach. Second, since the priests were responsible for interceding to God on behalf of the people, it would have been the height of disrespect to God to serve in the temple while intoxicated. God communicates His disgust concerning this abominable behavior of the priests in Isaiah's day:

> "Now, however, Israel is being led by drunks! The priests and prophets reel and stagger from beer and wine. They make stupid mistakes as they carry out their responsibilities." Isaiah 28:7, NLT

Third, the priests had to use great care when performing their tasks in the temple because they could literally be stricken dead by God if they were careless in His presence. We read of this happening to Aaron's sons in Leviticus 10:1–2. Foolishly, after allowing the fire to go out that God had miraculously provided in the altar of sacrifice (something the priests were warned not to do), Nadab and Abihu tried to compensate for their dereliction of duty by building a new, man-made fire in its place. For this, they incurred the judgment of God and paid with their lives. Even though the Bible says nothing about Nadab and Abihu being intoxicated, imagine how the potential for this type of mistake in the temple would have been significantly increased if the priests regularly drank fermented wine.

- Rulers were prohibited from drinking alcohol.

> "It is not for kings, O Lemuel—not for kings to drink wine, not for rulers to crave beer, lest they drink and forget what the law decrees, and deprive all the oppressed of their rights." Proverbs 31:4–5, NIV

It is easy to imagine why God forbade rulers to drink. The decisions that rulers have to make are too important for their minds to be clouded by alcohol. Imagine the President of the United States with his finger on the trigger of nuclear missiles, making world impacting decisions under the influence of alcohol. Consider members of our Congress making laws that drastically affect our lives while being held sway by the effects of liquor.

- Those who took a Nazirite vow were prohibited from drinking alcohol.

> "If some of the people, either men or women, take the special vow of a Nazirite, setting themselves apart to the LORD in a special way, they must give up wine and other alcoholic drinks. They must not use vinegar made from wine, they must not drink other fermented drinks or fresh grape juice, and they must not eat grapes or raisins. As long as they are bound by their Nazirite vow, they are not allowed to eat or drink anything that comes from a grapevine, not even the grape seeds or skins." Numbers 6:2–4, NLT

Those who had taken the Nazirite vow had been set aside for a special work for God. They were not allowed to drink anything alcoholic, nor could they even eat the fruit used to make wine. The famous strong man, Samson, had taken a Nazirite vow. This is why his mother was forbidden to drink wine while she carried him in her womb (Judges 13:3–4). This illustrates how important it was for believers to stay away from the defilement of alcohol if they desired to be used by God in a special way.

Although God never completely forbade Old Testament believers from drinking alcoholic wines, it is obvious that He intended that its use would be limited.

> "Do not gaze at wine when it is red, when it sparkles in the cup, when it goes down smoothly!" Proverbs 23:31, NLT

If God forbade the Jews to gaze at (desire or lust after) alcohol, it seems obvious to me that this prohibition would have included drinking it also.

REASONS GOD DID NOT INTEND FOR HIS PEOPLE TO REGULARLY DRINK ALCOHOL:

1. Wine drinking indicates a lack of wisdom.

> "Whoever is led astray by drink cannot be wise." Proverbs 20:1, NLT

"Alcohol and prostitution have robbed my people of their brains." Hosea 4:11, NLT

2. Wine leads to poverty.

"Do not carouse with drunkards and gluttons, for they are on their way to poverty." Proverbs 23:20–21, NLT

3. Wine produces mockers.

"Wine produces mockers . . ." Proverbs 20:1, NLT

4. Wine produces arrogance.

"Destruction is certain for those who are heroes when it comes to drinking, who boast about all the liquor they can hold." Isaiah 5:22, NLT

"See, he is puffed up; his desires are not upright—but the righteous will live by his faith—indeed, wine betrays him; he is arrogant and never at rest." Habakkuk 2:4–5, NLT

5. Wine takes purpose from life.

"Woe to those who rise early in the morning to run after their drinks, who stay up late at night till they are inflamed with wine." Isaiah 5:11, NIV

6. Wine takes away the senses.

"Your eyes will see strange sights and your mind imagine confusing things. You will be like one sleeping on the high seas, lying on top of the rigging. 'They hit me,' you will say, 'but I'm not hurt! They beat me, but I don't feel it! When will I wake up so I can find another drink?'" Proverbs 23:33–35, NIV

7. Wine causes disagreeableness.

"Who has strife? Who has complaints? Who has needless bruises? Who has bloodshot eyes? Those who linger over wine, who go to sample bowls of mixed wine." Proverbs 23:29–30, NIV

8. Wine causes quarrels.

" . . . liquor leads to brawls." Proverbs 20:1, NLT

"They . . . drink the wine of violence." Proverbs 4:17, NIV

"Who is always fighting . . . Who has unnecessary bruises . . . and you will say, 'They hit me, but I didn't feel it. I didn't even know it when they beat me up. When will I wake up so I can have another drink?'" Proverbs 23:29, 35, NLT

9. Wine brings anguish and sorrow.

"Who has woe? Who has sorrow? Who has strife? Who has complaints? Who has needless bruises? Who has bloodshot eyes? Those who linger over wine, who go to sample bowls of mixed wine." Proverbs 23:29, 30 NIV

10. Wine brings personal harms of all kinds.

" . . . For in the end it bites like a poisonous serpent; it stings like a viper." Proverbs 23:32, NLT

11. Wine lowers moral inhibitions.

"And your heart will utter perverse things." Proverbs 23:33, NKJV

Even though the Bible clearly condemns drunkenness, it seems to stop short of totally banning the use of fermented wines. Why? Dr. Ed Rickard offers some helpful insight:

"[People] in Bible times lived in countries where grapes were a principal source of food, and food was not always easy to come by. Many Israelites and Jews of antiquity were rural farmers, barely able to keep themselves at the level of subsistence. A merciful God, desiring His people to be adequately nourished, was not willing to deny them the use of any naturally abundant produce of their fields and hillsides. Therefore, he did not forbid grapes or grape juice or even fermented wine. He foresaw that in a time of scarcity, fermented wine might be about the only food available . . . Methods for preserving unfermented juice required some technical know-how and perhaps some additional cost. Therefore, to ease the burden on all His people, and to avoid putting the poor and unlearned at a disadvantage before the law, the Lord permitted the drinking of fermented wine . . . The Lord is always reticent to set down a law that will be generally ignored. Such a law, saving few from an evil practice but implicating many in disobedience, actually increases sin. Thus, because the Israelites would not heed a law against divorce, the Mosaic code permitted divorce under certain conditions (Matt. 19:7–8). Yet God so imprinted His hatred of divorce upon the Bible that any reader of tender conscience would not fail to see it. Similarly, in recognition of the hardness of the human heart, the Bible does not plainly prohibit the drinking of fermented wine. In ancient times, especially, such a ban would have gained little compliance. Yet the Lord has carefully salted His Word with many clues that His perfect will for the believer, especially for the believer in our day, is total abstinence."[135]

Even though the argument may be made that God allowed the use of alcohol in some instances, it is obvious that He, knowing its power to steal away that which is good, greatly limited its use. Ultimately, alcohol is a thief. It robs us of our morals, our minds, our peace, our happiness, and our purpose. It makes us disagreeable, involving us in meaningless quarrels. It causes all of this and much, much more. How can anyone see any real benefit in drinking it—even in small, moderate amounts? Just as God forbade its use in Old Testament times, I believe He also forbids its use in New Testament times as well.

But you may be asking, "Didn't Jesus drink fermented wine? Didn't He even make fermented wine?" Many think so, let's take a look . . .

Chapter 8

WAS JESUS A BOOZER?

JESUS AND SIN

"Hey, Jesus drank, so why's it wrong for me to drink? After all, I'm just doing what Jesus did." If only I had a dollar for every time I've heard someone say something like that. It is very disturbing for me to hear people carelessly accusing the Lord of condoning and even using alcoholic beverages that bring such devastation to millions. When evaluating the character, comments, and conduct of Jesus, we must show the utmost caution and reverence, keeping foremost in our minds that we are speaking of the sinless Son of God, the Creator of the universe, the Savior and Judge of all mankind. We must never "use" Jesus as an excuse for our own morally questionable practices.

It is essential that we keep in mind that from eternity past, Jesus was the sinless Son of God. In His incarnation, having no earthly father from whom He would have inherited a sinful nature, He remained sinless. This is explicitly stated in Scripture:

> "In the beginning the Word already existed. He was with God, and he was God. He was in the beginning with God. He created everything there is. Nothing exists that he didn't make . . . So the Word became human and lived here on earth among us. He was full of unfailing love and faithfulness. And we have seen his glory, the glory of the only Son of the Father." John 1:1–3, 14, NLT

> "'How will this be,' Mary asked the angel, 'since I am a virgin?' The angel answered, 'The Holy Spirit will come upon you, and the power of the Most High will overshadow you. So the holy one to be born will be called the Son of God.'" Luke 1:34–35, NIV

"For we do not have a high priest who is unable to sympathize with our weaknesses, but we have one who has been tempted in every way, just as we are—yet was without sin." Hebrews 4:15, NIV

Unlike you and me, Jesus didn't have a sinful nature for Satan to "get hold of" when tempting him. Jesus verified this when he said:

"I will not speak with you much longer, for the prince of this world is coming. He has no hold on me," John 14:30, NIV

In addition, the book of James teaches that God cannot be tempted to do wrong:

"God is never tempted to do wrong, and he never tempts anyone else either. Temptation comes from the lure of our own evil desires. These evil desires lead to evil actions, and evil actions lead to death." James 1:13–15, NLT

Since Jesus is God the Son, He cannot be tempted to sin. Although Satan tried (Matthew 4), he failed. Unlike Jesus, our temptations are given force by our own evil desires. As we act upon these desires, we sin and suffer the consequences.

It was imperative that Jesus not only be sinless, but that He remain so. Only a flawless, sinless sacrifice could pay for man's sins.

"When anyone brings from the herd or flock a fellowship offering to the LORD to fulfill a special vow or as a freewill offering, it must be without defect or blemish to be acceptable." Leviticus 22:21, NIV

"Without the shedding of blood, there is no forgiveness of sins. That is why the earthly tent [tabernacle] and everything in it—which were copies of things in heaven—had to be purified by the blood of animals. But the real things in heaven had to be purified with far better sacrifices than the blood of animals [the blood of Jesus]." Hebrews 9:22–24, NLT

"For it is not possible for the blood of bulls and goats to take away sins. That is why Christ, when he came into the world, said, 'You did not want animal sacrifices and grain offerings. But you have given me a body so that I may obey you.'" Hebrews 10:4–5, NLT

Thankfully, Jesus was a perfect sacrifice. Summarizing His atoning work on our behalf, Scripture says:

> "God made him [Jesus] who had no sin to be sin for us, so that in him [Jesus] we might become the righteousness of God." 2 Corinthians 5:21, NIV

> "so also Christ died only once as a sacrifice to take away the sins of many people." Hebrews 9:28, NLT

> "For you know that it was not with perishable things such as silver or gold that you were redeemed from the empty way of life handed down to you from your forefathers, but with the precious blood of Christ, a lamb without blemish or defect." 1 Peter 1:18–19, NIV

Even Judas recognized that Jesus was innocent:

> "When Judas, who had betrayed him, saw that Jesus was condemned, he was seized with remorse and returned the thirty silver coins to the chief priests and the elders. 'I have sinned,' he said, 'for I have betrayed innocent blood.'" Matthew 27:3–4, NIV

This is why accusing Jesus of condoning or committing any type of sin is such a serious matter. To imply that Jesus, our great High Priest (remember priests were forbidden to drink alcohol), participated in anything sinful is paramount to blasphemy. Look at it like this: if Jesus sinned, He was less than God, if He was less than God, He was less than Savior, and if He was less than Savior, then those who trust in Him are less than saved!

A GLUTTON & A DRUNKARD?

Those in His day hurled numerous and constant accusations against Jesus. One such accusation was that he was a glutton and a drunkard. In Matthew 11 we read:

> "For John the Baptist didn't drink wine and he often fasted, and you say, 'He's demon possessed.' And I, the Son of Man, feast and drink, and you say, 'He's a glutton and a drunkard, and a friend of the worst sort of sinners!' But wisdom is shown to be right by what results from it." Matthew 11:18–19, NLT

Those who favor drinking normally latch on to this passage and use it as a "proof text" for their right to drink. According to them, since this passage teaches that Jesus drank intoxicating wines, so can they. Does their interpretation square with the core message of this passage? No!

Rather than encouraging the consumption of alcohol, in Matthew 11:18–19 Jesus was pointing out the ingratitude of the Jews of his day. They had a habit of being dissatisfied with everything God did for them. As proof, they had rejected practically every prophet He had sent them. This is clearly expressed in verses 16 & 17:

> "How shall I describe this generation? These people are like a group of children playing a game in the public square. They complain to their friends, 'We played wedding songs, and you weren't happy, so we played funeral songs, but you weren't sad.'" Matthew 11:16–17, NLT

Because John the Baptist was a Nazirite, he conformed to the rigid requirements of the Nazirite vow given in Numbers 6:2–4. When the Jews saw his abstinence from all wines (fermented and unfermented), when they saw his uncommon appearance, and when they heard his strong call for repentance, they were extremely displeased and rejected him as a prophet of God. Their assessment of John is found in Matthew 11:18 where they said, "He's demon possessed." Similarly, when the hypocritical, wicked Pharisees who considered themselves too "spiritual" to stoop to the level of fellowshipping with "sinners," saw Jesus, whose mission was far different from John's, freely mingling with sinners, they called him a "glutton and a drunkard, and a friend of the worst sort of sinners!"

Before we jump to the conclusion that these Jewish critics were correct, we should remember that they also accused Jesus of being a glutton. Seldom, if ever, have I heard the proponents of drinking use this passage to justify gluttony. So why do they use it to justify drinking? This is extremely inconsistent. Hank Hanegraaff, President of the Christian Research Institute and host of the nationally aired "The Bible Answer Man" radio program, has coined a phrase for this type of Bible interpretation: he calls it "scrip-torture." According to Hank, "scrip-torture" is the practice of slicing and dicing the Scriptures, using only the parts needed to prove a point that is biblically inconsistent and incorrect.

We must not forget that in John 7:20, 8:48, and 10:20 these same Jews (those Jesus condemned as hypocrites in Matthew 23:13–39) accused Jesus of being demon possessed and crazy. Certainly we know that Jesus was neither possessed nor crazy—so why would we believe their accusation that He was a glutton and a drunkard? Recognizing now, that many of the wines of Jesus' day were unfermented, is there the slightest possibility that the wine He drank was unfermented? Of course there is! Dr. John J. Owen said:

> "As wine was a common beverage in that land of vineyards, in its unfermented state, our Lord most likely drank it."[136]

Those who use this Scripture to teach that Jesus drank alcohol can't have it both ways. If they're going to accept the Jews' accusation that Jesus was a drunkard or at least one who frequently drank intoxicating wines, then they must also accept the accusations that He was demon possessed, crazy, and a glutton! They can't take one accusation without taking the others.

Worth noting is Jesus' response to their accusation. He simply said, "But wisdom is shown to be right by what results from it." In other words, His words and works would prove His true character and defend Him against false accusations like these. Abraham Lincoln responded similarly when he was the target of severe criticism:

> "If I were to try to read, much less answer, all the attacks made on me, this shop might as well be closed for any other business. I do the very best I know how—the very best I can; and I mean to keep doing so until the end. If the end brings me out all right, what's said against me won't amount to anything. If the end brings me out wrong, ten angels swearing I was right would make no difference."[137]

On the day of Pentecost, the Apostle Peter confirmed that Jesus' words and works were indeed sufficient evidence of His divinity:

> "Men of Israel, listen to this: Jesus of Nazareth was a man accredited by God to you by miracles, wonders and signs, which God did among you through him, as you yourselves know . . . Therefore let all Israel be assured of this: God has made this Jesus, whom you crucified, both Lord and Christ." Acts 2:22, 36, NIV

Jesus' practice of spending time with notorious sinners is properly understood if we consider the primary goal of His mission. In Luke 19:10, Jesus said He came to "seek and to save those who were lost." Additionally, in Matthew 15:24, He said that He was sent to the "lost sheep of Israel." The reason Jesus spent so much time around sinners was because He loved them and desired to redeem them. When challenged by the Jews concerning this practice, He said, "It is not the healthy who need a doctor, but the sick. For I have not come to call the righteous, but sinners." Luke 5:31–31, NIV.

This does not mean that He condoned or committed their sins in order to relate to them. Instead, by befriending them, He was able to win their trust and reach through the sin to the sinner. If the accusation that Jesus actually practiced their sins is true, then how could He be their "spiritual physician?" If He, the physician, suffered from the same (spiritual) illness, how could He successfully treat His patients? If the Savior practiced the sins of the sinners, how could He call them to repentance seeing that He too was guilty? Not many years later, Paul used this same outreach strategy in attempting to reach those in his circle of influence:

> "When I am with the Jews, I become one of them so that I can bring them to Christ. When I am with those who follow the Jewish laws, I do the same, even though I am not subject to the law, so that I can bring them to Christ. When I am with the Gentiles who do not have the Jewish law, I fit in with them as much as I can. In this way, I gain their confidence and bring them to Christ. But I do not discard the law of God; I obey the law of Christ. When I am with those who are oppressed, I share their oppression so that I might bring them to

Christ. Yes, I try to find common ground with everyone so that I might bring them to Christ." 1 Corinthians 9:20–22, NLT

Are we to assume from Paul's words that he indulged in the sinful practices of those he was attempting to reach in order to relate to them? Or, was he saying that he was willing to do whatever was necessary, within biblical parameters, to win as many people to Christ as possible? I am convinced it was the latter.

THE "KEGGER AT CANA"

Another passage popular with those who advocate drinking is John 2:1–11 which tells the story of Jesus turning water into wine at a marriage celebration in Cana of Galilee. For many, this is the "mother lode" proving that Jesus condoned the use of intoxicating, fermented wine. Those desperate to find a biblical concession for drinking alcoholic beverages automatically assume that the wine Jesus made was fermented—even though there is nothing in the text that implies this. Yes, the master of the feast comments that the wine Jesus made was better than that which had been served earlier, but this does not mean it was fermented—it just means that it was better. It is helpful to remember that we have already seen that the people of Jesus' day preferred the taste of sweet, unfermented wines over those that were fermented. So it is reasonable to suggest, at least, that the wines being served at the wedding were quite possibly unfermented.

The text of John 2:1–11 reads:

"The next day Jesus' mother was a guest at a wedding celebration in the village of Cana in Galilee. Jesus and his disciples were also invited to the celebration. The wine supply ran out during the festivities, so Jesus' mother spoke to him about the problem. 'They have no more wine,' she told him. 'How does that concern you and me?' Jesus asked. 'My time has not yet come.' But his mother told the servants, 'Do whatever he tells you.' Six stone water pots were standing there; they were used for Jewish ceremonial purposes and held twenty to thirty gallons each. Jesus told the servants, 'Fill the jars with water.' When the jars had been filled to the brim, he said, 'Dip some out and take it to the master of ceremonies.' So they followed his instructions. When the master of ceremonies tasted the water that was now wine, not knowing where it had come from (though, of course, the servants knew), he called the bridegroom over. 'Usually a host serves the best wine first,' he said. 'Then, when everyone is full and doesn't care, he brings out the less expensive wines. But you have kept the best until now!' This miraculous sign at Cana in Galilee was Jesus' first display of his glory. And his disciples believed in him." John 2:1–11, NLT

Since the advocates of drinking automatically assume that the wine being served at the wedding feast was fermented, they assume that the wine Jesus made was fermented also. Yet, is there anything in this text that would lead them to this conclusion? The only reason I can see is a presupposition that drinking fermented wine is acceptable. This supposition apparently drives them to attempt to find in Jesus' actions justification for their own choice to drink.

Since the word translated wine in this passage is the Greek word *oinos,* it can be referring to either fermented or unfermented wine. Therefore the only way to determine which kind of wine Jesus made is to take a serious look at the context of the passage.

I concur with Dr. William Patton who said that the dilemma of whether or not the wine Jesus made was fermented is easily solved by considering the three main parts of the miracle: the occasion, the material used, and the performer of the miracle.[138] By considering these three parts in greater detail, I believe we can easily determine what type of wine Jesus made.

One: The occasion of the miracle was the wedding celebration of a Jewish couple. First, we must understand that the wedding feast was a very important event in the Jewish culture and was usually a momentous celebration. These celebrations were greatly anticipated and well attended, so it is natural that Jesus and his disciples would attend. Jesus even used the Jewish wedding feast to illustrate the future kingdom of God (Matt. 22:2–14, 25:1–13, Rev. 19:7–9). The important question to ask is: "Did Jews routinely drink fermented wine at their wedding celebrations?" Dr. S.

M. Isaacs, a Jewish rabbi who lived in New York City in the 19th century, wrote:

> "In the Holy Land they do not commonly use fermented wines. The best wines are preserved sweet and unfermented . . . The Jews do not, in their feasts for sacred purposes, **including the marriage feast**, ever use any kind of fermented drinks. In their oblations and libations, both private and public, they employ the fruit of the vine—that is, fresh grapes—unfermented grape juice, and raisins, as the symbol of benediction. Fermentation is to them always a symbol of corruption, as in nature and science it is itself decay, rottenness."[139]

Since the Bible speaks so negatively of fermented wine and since, according to Dr. Isaacs, the **religious** Jews did not traditionally use fermented wines at their wedding celebrations, I'm convinced that it is most probable that the wine being served at the marriage in Cana would have been unfermented. But regardless of which kind of wine had been served at the wedding before Jesus performed His miracle, I'm convinced that He did not make fermented wine.

Two: The material used in performing this miracle was water. The text informs us that Jesus specifically instructed them to fill six pots (which held approximately twenty to thirty gallons each) with water. From this pure water, Jesus miraculously made 120–180 gallons of wine. Commenting on this, Dr. Patton wrote:

> "Christ did instantly what, by the laws of nature which he had ordained, it would have taken months to grow and ripen into [its final fruit]. So in the case of the wine, Christ, by supernatural and superhuman rapidity, produced that marvelous conversion of water into the 'pure blood of the grape' which, by his own established law of nature, takes place annually through a series of months, as the vine draws up the water from the earth, and transmutes it into the pure and unfermented juice found in the rich, ripe clusters on the vine."[140]

In essence, this is what Psalms 104:14–15 says: "He [God] makes grass grow for the cattle, and plants for man to cultivate—bringing forth food from the earth: wine that gladdens the heart of man," NIV. In simple terms, water is drawn up from the ground by the roots of the vine and is then transformed by the vine into grape juice in the grape. St. Augustine, an early Christian leader, born in 354 A.D., wrote:

> "For he on that marriage day made wine in the six jars which he ordered to be filled with water—he who now makes it every year in the vines; for, as what the servants had poured into the water jars was turned into wine by the power of the Lord, so, also, that which the clouds pour forth is turned into wine by the power of the self-same Lord. But we cease to wonder at what is done every year; its very frequency makes astonishment to fail."[141]

Chrysostom, another early Christian leader, born in 344 A.D., wrote:

> "Now, indeed, making plain that it is he who changes into wine the water in the vines and the rain drawn up by the roots. He produced instantly at the wedding feast that which is formed in the plant during a long course of time."[142]

It would seem consistent with His nature as Creator, that Jesus would, in turning water into wine, replicate the natural process He created in the first place. The idea that He would make fermented wine goes against nature and logic. Sir Humphry Davy wrote of alcohol, "It has never been found ready formed in plants," and Count Chaptal, the French chemist declared, "Nature never forms spirituous liquors; she rots the grape upon the branch, but it is art which converts the juice into (alcoholic) wine."[143] Dr. Henry Monroe in his *Lecture on Alcohol* wrote: "Alcohol is nowhere to be found in any product of nature; was never created by God; but is essentially an artificial thing prepared by man through the destructive process of fermentation."[144] Since fermented wine does not occur naturally, but is man-made and contributes greatly to his misery, I am convinced Jesus would have only made unfermented wine at the wedding feast.

Three: The one who performed this miracle was the Lord Jesus. Consider this: would Jesus have done anything inconsistent with his holy character? John R. Rice responds to this question in his verse by verse commentary of the Gospel of John:

> "You may be sure that Jesus knew well the teaching that 'wine is a mocker, strong drink is raging,' and he would not go against the teaching of scripture of which he himself was author and founder before the world began. The kind of wine which Jesus made is not the kind which is a mocker and, along with strong drink, is raging."[145]

Dr. William Patton adds these comments:

> "Is it not derogatory to the character of Christ and the teachings of the Bible to suppose that he exerted his miraculous power to produce . . . at least 60 gallons of intoxicating wine?—wine which inspiration had denounced as 'a mocker,' as 'biting like a serpent,' and 'stinging like an adder,' as 'the poison of dragons,' 'the cruel venom of asps,' and which the Holy Ghost had selected as the emblem of the wrath of God Almighty? Is it probable that he gave that to the guests after they had used the wine provided by the host, and which, it is claimed, was intoxicating?"[146]

Dr. R.A. Torrey, the great theologian, wrote in 1907:

> "The wine provided for in the marriage festivities at Cana failed. A cloud was about to fall over the joy of what is properly a festive occasion. Jesus came to the rescue. He provided wine, but there is not a hint that the wine he made was intoxicating. It was fresh-made wine. New-made wine is never intoxicating. It is not intoxicating until sometime after the process of fermentation has set in. Fermentation is a process of decay. There is not a hint that our Lord produced alcohol, which is a product of decay or death. He produced a living wine uncontaminated by fermentation."[147]

The Bible scholar, Dr. William Pettingill, wrote:

> "I do not pretend to know the nature of the wine furnished by our Lord at the wedding of Cana, but I am satisfied that there was little resemblance in it to the thing described in the Scriptures of God as biting like a serpent and stinging like an adder (Prov. 23:29–32). Doubtless rather it was like the heavenly fruit of the vine that he will drink new with his own in his Father's kingdom (Matt. 26:29). No wonder the governor of the wedding feast at Cana pronounced it the best wine

kept until the last. Never before had he tasted such wine, and never did he taste it again."[148]

In the miracle at Cana, I am convinced that Jesus acted in a way consistent with His character. Like the scholars I have just quoted, I find it beyond all reasonable comprehension that Jesus would have made and offered to the wedding guests at Cana, a beverage that was capable of such injury, grief, and damnation as alcohol. Jesus' half-brother, James, reminds us in James 1:17 that only good things come from God: "Every good and perfect gift is from above, coming down from the Father of the heavenly lights, who does not change like shifting shadows." NIV, and as we have seen, alcohol is generally not a good thing. He also reminds us in James 1:13 that God never tempts us to sin. If Jesus had given intoxicating wine to the guests at Cana, then He would have been offering something to them that would tempt them to sin (Prov. 23:29–35) and which would have been contradictory to His own teaching in Matthew 6:13 where He taught His followers to pray that God would not, "lead them into temptation, but deliver them from the evil one."

Finally, was this first miracle only a casual, flippant use of Jesus' power just to satisfy His mother and a crowd's thirst for liquor, or did it have some special significance? If one looks closely, he will find that the Bible highlights this, the first of Jesus' miracles, as special among all of the miracles He performed. Dr. Gerald L. Borchert, Director of Doctoral Studies and Professor of New Testament at Northern Baptist Theological Seminary comments:

> "The positioning of this sign in the Gospel obviously is of crucial importance because it is not merely intended to be the first (by number) of such miraculous events but also functions as the head, clue, or key to the signs of Jesus (John 2:11). The one who understands this sign should understand the point of all the signs."[149]

Since the purpose of this miracle was not, as many believe, to give Jesus an opportunity to condone the use of alcoholic beverages, then what was its purpose? John 2:11 says, "This miraculous sign at Cana in Galilee was Jesus' first display of his glory. And his disciples believed in him," NLT. According to Scripture, it was performed to give Jesus an opportunity to display His glory as the true Son of God. After witnessing this miracle firsthand, the disciples were encouraged to believe that He was the Creator seeing He had power over the elements. Thus, this miracle was not performed to give believers an excuse to drink alcohol but to give them a reason to believe in the divinity of Christ!

So if the wine Jesus made was not fermented, what kind of wine was it? Like Dr. Pettingill, I believe Jesus probably gave those present at the wedding a preview of what the saints will drink in God's future kingdom. In other words, what He made was "kingdom wine." This is probably why the master of the feast was so "blown away" by its quality. The Old Testament prophet, Joel, in writing about the future kingdom of God, wrote:

> "In that day the mountains will drip with sweet wine, and the hills will flow with milk. Water will fill the dry streambeds of Judah, and a fountain will burst forth from the Lord's Temple, watering the arid valley of acacias." Joel 3:18, NLT

Jesus told His disciples at the "Last Supper" that He would drink wine with them in the coming kingdom of God:

> "Mark my words—I will not drink wine again until the day I drink it new with you in my Father's Kingdom." Matthew 26:29, NLT

If this means that believers will drink wine in God's eternal kingdom, then it is inconceivable that this wine will be fermented; especially since Revelation 21:27 says: "Nothing impure will ever enter it [God's kingdom]," NIV. Whatever this wine will be, I am certain it will not be a beverage that will have the capability of turning the redeemed saints into eternal drunks!

NEW WINE AND OLD SKINS

Another passage often used to teach that Jesus condoned

the use of alcohol is found in Matthew 9 (also Mark 2:22 & Luke 5:37). In this Scripture, Jesus says:

> "And no one puts new wine into old wineskins. The old skins would burst from the pressure, spilling the wine and ruining the skins. New wine must be stored in new wineskins. That way both the wine and the wineskins are preserved." Matthew 9:17, NLT

No doubt, Jesus used this illustration because it was something to which the people of His day could relate. To properly understand Jesus' statement, we must first notice that He referred to new wine, making an obvious distinction between new (unfermented) and old (fermented) wine. Jesus was saying that if new wine was stored in old wineskins (containers that had previously held wine) there was the real risk that the old wineskins could burst and spill out the new wine. Have you ever wondered why the old wineskins had such a tendency to burst? Consider that the old wineskins would have contained decaying remnants of wine that had previously been stored in them. These decaying remnants of old wine would have acted as yeast and would have begun the fermentation process in the new wine. The fermentation that would have occurred inside these old wineskins would not only have ruined the new wine, but would have released carbonic gas causing the brittle skins to swell and rupture allowing the wine to spill out. In the 1750 work, *Chamber's Cyclopedia,* we find:

> "The force of fermenting wine is very great, being able, if closely stopped up, to burst through the strongest cask"[150]

This is what Job 32:18–19 is referring to:

> "For I am pent up and full of words, and the spirit within me urges me on. I am like a wine cask without a vent. My words are ready to burst out!" Job 32:18–19, NLT

In the work, *Greek and Roman Antiquities,* we find this helpful information:

> "When it was desired to preserve a quantity in the sweet state, an

amphora [container] was taken and coated with pitch [sealant] within and without; it was filled with the mustum lixivium [fruit juice—normally grape], and corked, so as to be perfectly air-tight."[151]

Commenting on this, Dr. William Patton wrote that it was not so much the weakened state of the old wineskins that concerned the people, but the contamination of the new wine:

> "I have said, if the 'new wine' had already fermented, the old bottles would suit just as well as the new; but, if not fermented, the old would not suit, not because they were weak, but because they would have portions of the albuminous [protein] matter or yeast adhering to the sides. This, having absorbed oxygen from the air, would become active fermenting matter, and would communicate it to the entire mass . . . The new bottles or skins, being clean and perfectly free from all ferment, were essential for preserving the fresh unfermented juice, not that their strength might resist the force of fermentation, but, being clean and free from fermenting matter, and closely tied and sealed, so as to exclude the air, the wine would be preserved in the same state in which it was when put into those skins."[152]

We must understand that Jesus was not using this illustration to encourage the consumption of fermented wines. In fact, Jesus wasn't even making a statement about drinking wines at all; He was simply using wine and wineskins to illustrate a spiritual truth. By reading verses 14–16 this becomes clear:

> "One day the disciples of John the Baptist came to Jesus and asked him, 'Why do we and the Pharisees fast, but your disciples don't fast?' Jesus responded, 'Should the wedding guests mourn while celebrating with the groom? Someday he will be taken from them, and then they will fast. And who would patch an old garment with unshrunk cloth? For the patch shrinks and pulls away from the old cloth, leaving an even bigger hole than before.'" Matthew 9:14–16, NLT

John MacArthur's commentary on this passage is extremely helpful:

> "But an even more important issue was behind the question of John's disciples. Since they obviously had not become disciples of Jesus as John had instructed them to do, they had no basis for genuine faith.

But it was clear to them, as it was to the Pharisees, that Jesus' teaching and activities were radically different from those of traditional Judaism. Consequently, behind their question about fasting may have been a deeper concern about forgiveness. 'Why,' they may really have been wondering, 'do You emphasize internal things such as forgiveness, while our recognized religious leaders only emphasize external things such as fasting?'

Jesus' next two illustrations deal with that issue. He made it clear that He was not teaching a reformed Pharisaism or a reformed rabbinicalism but an entirely different way of believing, thinking, and living. He did not come to improve the old system but to renounce and undermine it. His way had nothing to do with the old ways, and the old ways had no part in the new. The two ways cannot be connected to one another or be contained in the other . . . In the same way, Jesus' new and internal gospel of forgiveness and cleansing cannot be attached to the old and external traditions of self-righteousness and ritual."[153]

In simple terms: Jesus was teaching that salvation is not a matter of religion and outward works (old wineskins), but is a matter of a relationship with God made possible by a transformed life through the new birth (new wine). The new wine of salvation by faith in Jesus' death and resurrection could not function within the old wineskins of the Law. This illustration of the new wine and old wineskins has nothing to do with condoning the use of alcoholic beverages.

THE WINE AT THE LAST SUPPER

Jesus was crucified during the Jewish feast of Passover. Most know that the first Passover occurred in Egypt when God sent the last plague of judgment upon Pharaoh and the Egyptians. The complete story can be found in Exodus 12. The Jews were to kill a lamb and place its blood on the doorposts and lintels of their houses. When the death angel came through the land, he would "pass over" every house where the blood had been applied. The Jews were also instructed to prepare a meal of bitter herbs and unleavened bread signifying their bitter bondage and the haste with which they would leave Egypt. This ceremony became a special memorial feast the Jews celebrated every year. Though literal, the Passover ceremony was also prophetic of a greater deliverance—the deliverance from the bondage of sin ultimately provided by Jesus, the Lamb of God, slain for the sins of all mankind.

On the night before Jesus was crucified, He celebrated Passover with His disciples. It was during this "last supper" that He explained the true meaning of the elements of Passover to His disciples, forever transforming the feast into a memorial of His death on the cross that would be celebrated perpetually by His followers. We find the story in Matthew 26:

> "While they were eating, Jesus took bread, gave thanks and broke it, and gave it to his disciples, saying, 'Take and eat; this is my body.' Then he took the cup, gave thanks and offered it to them, saying, 'Drink from it, all of you. This is my blood of the covenant, which is poured out for many for the forgiveness of sins. I tell you, I will not drink of this fruit of the vine from now on until that day when I drink it anew with you in my Father's kingdom.'" Matthew 26:26–29, NIV

Jesus took the unleavened bread, gave thanks, broke it, gave it to the disciples, and told them that it now represented His sinless body which would be broken for them. Then He took the cup, gave thanks, gave it to the disciples to drink, and told them that it represented His sinless blood which would be poured out for the forgiveness of sins. It is here that some make an attempt to portray Jesus as a drinker of fermented wine by insisting that the wine He and His disciples drank at the supper was fermented. So, was it?

Let's begin by noting that the Bible uses leaven (yeast) as a symbol for sin. Matthew 16 illustrates this:

> "'Be careful,' Jesus said to them. 'Be on your guard against the yeast of the Pharisees and Sadducees.' They discussed this among themselves and said, 'It is because we didn't bring any bread.' Then they understood that he was not telling them to guard against the yeast used in bread, but against the teaching of the Pharisees and Sadducees." Matthew 16:6–7, 12, NIV

Paul made this same point as he wrote to the Corinthian believers about the sin they were allowing to go unpunished in their fellow-ship:

> "Your boasting is not good. Don't you know that a little yeast works through the whole batch of dough? Get rid of the old yeast that you may be a new batch without yeast—as you really are. For Christ, our Passover lamb, has been sacrificed. Therefore let us keep the Festival, not with the old yeast, the yeast of malice and wickedness, but with bread without yeast, the bread of sincerity and truth." 1 Corinthians 5:6–8, NIV

This is why God forbade leaven in any sacrifice offered in the Old Testament Law. In Exodus 34:25 we read: "Do not offer the blood of a sacrifice to me along with anything containing yeast," NIV. Sacrifices offered to the Lord had to be pure and unblemished and since yeast symbolized sin, the sacrifices couldn't contain any yeast. God told the Jews in Exodus 12 that they were to remove all yeast from their houses before celebrating Passover and that all elements of the Passover celebration must be yeast-free. All of this was done to symbolize the sanctity of the feast and to underline the need to keep it pure and free from the defilement of sin.

Why would we then assume that as Jesus and His disciples observed the Passover at the Last Supper, they would willfully sin by disobeying God's Law by using things containing yeast? Professor Moses Stuart wrote:

> "The Hebrew [forbids] anything fermented [in the Passover celebration]. All leaven, i.e. fermentation, was excluded from offerings to God."[154]

Dr. William Patton added:

> "The great mass of the Jews have ever understood this prohibition as extending to fermented wine, or strong drink, as well as to bread. The word is essentially the same which designates the fermentation of bread as that of liquors."[155]

Gesenius, the Hebrew scholar, declared: "Leaven applied to the wine as really as to the bread."[156] This means that the Jews considered both leavened (fermented) bread *and* fermented (leavened) wine unacceptable for use in the Passover celebration.

As we have already seen, the rabbi, Dr. S. M. Isaacs, claimed that the Jews did not use fermented wines in their sacred feasts, but instead used the fruit of the vine—fresh grape juice. In the 19th century, Dr. A. P. Peabody wrote:

> " . . . in our Savior's time the Jews, at least the high ritualists among them, extended the prohibition of leaven to the principle of fermentation in every form; and that it was customary, at the Passover festival, for the master of the household to press the contents of 'the cup' from clusters of grapes preserved for this special purpose."[157]

Once again, it seems inconceivable that Jesus would have used fermented (leavened) wine in His Passover celebration. Imagine the sinless Christ, who would never tempt anyone to sin, offering liquor to His disciples and then promoting it as the eternal symbol of His shed blood on the cross. We find this illuminating quote in *Bible Wines:*

> "All admit that the bread was unleavened—had not passed the putrefaction or fermentation—and was, therefore, the proper emblem of the body of Christ, which "saw no corruption" [Ps. 26:10 & Acts 2:31]. For the same reason, there was a necessity that the wine should be unfermented, that it might be the fit emblem of the great Sacrifice which "saw no corruption." . . . If leaven was not allowed with the sacrifices, which were the types of the atoning blood of Christ, how much more would it be a violation of the commandment to allow leaven, or that which was fermented, to be the symbol of the blood of atonement? We cannot imagine that our Lord, in disregard of so positive a command, would admit leaven into the element which was to perpetuate the memory of the sacrifice of himself, of which all the other sacrifices were but types. Our Lord blessed the bread, and for the cup he gave thanks. Each element alike was the occasion of devout blessing and thanksgiving. This cup contained that which the Savior, just about to offer, could bless, and which he, for all time, designated as the symbol of his own atoning blood . . . Is it probable that Christ took an intoxicating liquor, which in all the ages past had been the cause of misery and ruin, and which in all the ages to come would destroy myriads in

temporal and eternal destruction; . . . and made that the symbol of his atonement, saying, 'This is the New Testament in my blood?'"[158]

Since only unleavened bread could represent the sinless body of Jesus, only **unleavened** wine would be a fitting symbol of His sinless blood. Quite possibly Jesus, when referring to the cup as the "fruit of the vine" in Matthew 26:29, was thinking of Deuteronomy 32:14 which speaks of the "pure blood of the grape," which, of course, would be a perfect symbol for His own "pure blood." Rather than calling it wine which He knew would be interpreted by some to mean fermented wine, He referred to it as the juice that comes directly from the vine. Since, in the Lord's Supper, it represented His blood, it is only fitting that they used the pure blood of the grape—juice. This squares with Peter's words in 1 Peter 1:19 where he reminds us that we were redeemed with the "precious blood of the Lamb, without spot and without blemish," KJV. Fermented wine simply could not symbolize this "precious blood." Dr. W. A. Criswell, the famous pastor of the First Baptist Church in Dallas, Texas, wrote:

> "It is a very interesting thing to me as I study the Scriptures that at no time in the four accounts of the institution of the Lord's Supper is the word 'wine' used. Always it is called the 'cup' or the 'fruit of the vine' . . . The Lord knew all about that, and back in that day long ago when there was no possibility of keeping crushed fruit of the vine without its fermenting the Lord knew this day was coming, and He purposefully never used the word 'wine' but instead 'cup' or 'fruit of the vine.'"[159]

This belief was also held by the early church fathers. Clement, of Alexandria, in A.D. 180 wrote that the liquid used by Jesus at the "Last Supper" was "the blood of the vine," and Thomas Aquinas indicated: "Grape juice has the specific quality of wine, and, therefore, this sacrament may be celebrated with grape juice."[160] It seems clear to me that the wine Jesus and His disciples used at the Last Supper was undoubtedly unfermented.

THE WINE OFFERED TO JESUS
ON THE CROSS

It was a custom in Jesus' day to offer those being crucified a crude mixture of wine and gall. This drink was intended to ease the pain of the condemned. While on the cross, Jesus was also offered this drink. The Scriptures record:

> "One of them ran and filled a sponge with sour wine, holding it up to him on a stick so he could drink." Mark 15:36, NLT

> "The soldiers mocked him, too, by offering him a drink of sour wine." Luke 23:36, NLT

> "Jesus knew that everything was now finished, and to fulfill the Scriptures he said, 'I am thirsty.' A jar of sour wine was sitting there, so they soaked a sponge in it, put it on a hyssop branch, and held it up to his lips. When Jesus had tasted it, he said, 'It is finished!' Then he bowed his head and gave up his spirit." John 19:28–30, NLT

These verses serve as a good example of how we must interpret the Bible holistically. If only the above passages are read, one could make the argument that even though the Scriptures do not explicitly state it, it appears that Jesus may have drunk the wine given to Him while He was on the cross. But, the next passage ends all debate.

> "The soldiers gave him wine mixed with bitter gall, but when he had tasted it, he refused to drink it." Matthew 27:34, NLT

This passage decisively solves the dilemma. Jesus did not drink fermented wine—not even the wine offered to ease His pain on the cross.

One other point is worth noting. The Scriptures make it clear that Jesus, and only Jesus could purchase our salvation—no human work or assistance would do. Salvation was God's work and His alone. Therefore, Jesus wouldn't even accept the ancient alcoholic pain killer offered to him by the soldiers. It should impassion us to know that Christ bore the burden the entire way for us.

He took every blow, endured every insult, and felt every pain—all without the aid of any alcoholic anesthesia. In the book of Philippians, Paul emphasized this price that Jesus paid:

> "And being found in appearance as a man, he humbled himself and became obedient to death—even the death on a cross!" Philippians 2:8, NIV

Hallelujah! What a "sober" Savior!

Chapter 9

THE CHURCH AND THE BOTTLE

"These men are not drunk, as you suppose," Acts 2:15, NIV—
so responded Peter on the Day of Pentecost as the critical crowd
that had crucified Jesus mocked His followers. Their accusation is
found in verse 13: "Some, however, made fun of them and said,
'They have had too much wine [new wine, KJV],'" NIV. Can this
Scripture be used to prove that the early believers were in the habit
of drinking intoxicating wines?

Just as the Pharisees had rejected Jesus, accusing Him of
being demon possessed, so the same Jews rejected the Spirit's work
in Jesus' followers as well, insisting that they were drunk. The
Pharisees' accusation against Jesus' disciples was as bogus as were
their accusations against Jesus. Stop and think about the absurdity
of this accusation. Could drunkenness adequately explain how a
group of uneducated Galileans could speak in so many languages
as Acts 2 records?

> "Godly Jews from many nations were living in Jerusalem at that
> time. When they heard this sound, they came running to see what it
> was all about, and they were bewildered to hear their own languages
> being spoken by the believers.

> They were beside themselves with wonder. 'How can this be?' they
> exclaimed. 'These people are all from Galilee, and yet we hear them
> speaking the languages of the lands where we were born! Here we
> are—Parthians, Medes, Elamites, people from Mesopotamia, Judea,
> Cappadocia, Pontus, the province of Asia, Phrygia, Pamphylia, Egypt,
> and the areas of Libya toward Cyrene, visitors from Rome (both Jews
> and converts to Judaism), Cretans, and Arabians. And we all hear these

people speaking in our own languages about the wonderful things God has done!' They stood there amazed and perplexed. 'What can this mean?' they asked each other. But others in the crowd were mocking. 'They're drunk, that's all!' they said." Acts 2:5–13, NLT

How ridiculous for them to assume that liquor could transform common, uneducated men into scholars and linguists. Equally ridiculous is the fact that the mockers would assume that drunkenness could be achieved by drinking what was normally un-intoxicating wine (new wine—*gleukos*). In addition to this, even drunkards were not normally drunk as early in the morning as nine o'clock (Acts 2:15), the time the events in Acts 2 took place. In fact, Paul says that drunkards were normally drunk at night: "For those who sleep, sleep at night, and those who get drunk, get drunk at night," 1 Thessalonians 5:7, NIV. Given that wines in the New Testament were weak compared with today's wines, it is debatable whether or not it was even possible for a person to drink enough wine to get drunk this early in the day. In fact, it normally took a whole day of drinking these weak wines to get drunk, so a person had to intentionally drink huge quantities to get drunk.

As we have seen, it's unwise to base one's theology on the accusations of an ungodly crowd. The spiritual insight of a group of people who, just a few weeks before, had accused Jesus of being demon possessed is not very reliable.

WINE IN THE CHURCH AT CORINTH

Even though the believers on the Day of Pentecost were not guilty of drunkenness, believers later in the 1st century were. Sometime around 55–57 A.D., Paul wrote a letter (1 Corinthians) to the believers in Corinth correcting them, among numerous things, of their use of fermented wine. Paul's letter to these believers was a stinging rebuke directed at their unbiblical beliefs and practices. Corinth, situated right in the center of the Greek culture, was a collage of pagan religions. Those who had become Christ followers in Corinth had been saved out of a world of idolatry and paganism, making this church a virtual breeding bed of spiritual perversion and false teaching. Among their unbiblical practices was their use of fermented wines—especially in the celebration of the Lord's Supper. Paul addressed this in 1 Corinthians 11:

> "When you come together, it is not the Lord's Supper you eat, for as you eat, each of you goes ahead without waiting for anybody else. One remains hungry, another gets drunk." 1 Corinthians 11:20–21, NIV

The situation in the church at Corinth was deplorable. The rich and poor were coming together to celebrate the Lord's Supper but they were making a complete mockery of it. The rich were bringing food and wine with which they would gorge themselves and become drunk. While they were selfishly eating and drinking, the needs of the poor were being completely neglected causing them to often go away from the supper hungry and offended. Paul points out that this was not the purpose of the supper and that such desecration of it was blasphemous.

Since we have already seen that Jesus did not use fermented wine in the "Last Supper" or the first "Lord's Supper," the believers shouldn't have been using it in their observance of the Lord's Supper. Even though drinking and drunkenness had been a way of life for these Corinthians before coming to Christ, now that they were saved, Paul had nothing but rebuke for their continued drinking and gluttony:

> "What shall I say to you? Shall I praise you for this? Certainly not!" 1 Corinthians 11:22, NIV

As he reminds them of the purity, purpose, and practice of the Lord's Supper in verses 23–26, Paul gives no indication whatsoever, that fermented wine should have been used. In fact, in most translations, rather than calling it wine, he intentionally calls it "the cup" instead. In 1 Corinthians 10:16, Paul calls it the "cup of blessing." How could a cup of intoxicating wine capable of inducing such incredible perversion be considered a cup of blessing?

Paul wrote that the Corinthians' sin of desecrating the

Lord's Supper was so serious that in judgment, God had caused many of them to become sick and had allowed some of them to die:

> "Therefore, whoever eats the bread or drinks the cup of the Lord in an unworthy manner will be guilty of sinning against the body and blood of the Lord. A man ought to examine himself before he eats of the bread and drinks of the cup. For anyone who eats and drinks without recognizing the body of the Lord eats and drinks judgment on himself. That is why many among you are weak and sick, and a number of you have fallen asleep [died]. But if we judged ourselves, we would not come under judgment. When we are judged by the Lord, we are being disciplined so that we will not be condemned with the world." 1 Corinthians 11:27–32, NIV

Seeing that God acted so dramatically, how can anyone even suggest that this passage is proof that the use of alcohol was acceptable in the early church? The use of fermented wine in the church at Corinth produced sin, judgment, shame, and death and it's no different today.

TEMPERANCE AND MODERATION

But I can hear someone saying, "Hey, wait just one minute! Didn't Paul teach that believers should practice temperance and moderation?" Yes he did. But his teaching on temperance and moderation had nothing to do specifically with drinking alcohol. The following are the passages in the New Testament that speak of temperance and moderation (I have used the KJV since it uses the actual English words: temperance, temperate, & moderation):

- "And after certain days, when Felix came with his wife Drusilla, which was a Jewess, he sent for Paul, and heard him concerning the faith in Christ. And as he reasoned of righteousness, temperance [NIV: self-control], and judgment to come, Felix trembled, and answered, Go thy way for this time; when I have a convenient season, I will call for thee." Acts 24:24–25, KJV

This passage details Paul's visit with Felix, the Roman Governor, and his wife, Drusilla. According to the passage, Paul shared the Gospel with them and warned them that God demanded righteousness and temperance (self-control). He told them that they would someday face the judgment and would have to give an account to God for their lives. Paul's message was so strong that the Bible says Felix trembled. In this entire passage, there is absolutely nothing that even hints that Paul was talking about alcohol. Paul's reference to temperance had to do with living a godly, self-controlled life, not the moderate drinking of alcohol (although living a godly life would certainly involve controlling one's drinking). Since alcohol is not even mentioned, those who insist on using this passage to condone moderate drinking must resort to reading it into the text because it is simply not there.

- "But the fruit of the Spirit is love, joy, peace, longsuffering, gentleness, goodness, faith, meekness, temperance [NIV & NLT: self-control]: against such there is no law." Galatians 5:22–23, KJV

This passage details the godly characteristics that the Holy Spirit produces in the life of a believer. Again, temperance in this passage means self-control and is not a specific reference to drinking alcohol. It is also unthinkable to believe that Paul intended to teach that, along with love, joy, peace, and faith, one of the fruits that the Holy Spirit produces in the life of a believer is controlled drinking. I am convinced that any fair-minded, tender-hearted Bible student will not use this passage to encourage moderate drinking.

- "And beside this, giving all diligence, add to your faith virtue; and to virtue knowledge; and to knowledge temperance [NIV & NLT: self-control]; and to temperance patience; and to patience godliness; and to godliness brotherly kindness; and to brotherly kindness charity." 2 Peter 1:5–7, KJV

Here Peter is encouraging spiritual growth in the believer. Like Paul, he also uses the word temperance to refer to self-control. Again, there is no specific reference to alcohol in this passage and it is inconceivable that Peter intended to include (along with diligence, faith, virtue, and knowledge) controlled drinking as a mark of Christian maturity. So this passage is also not speaking of moderate drinking.

- "And every man that striveth for the mastery is temperate [NIV: goes into strict training & NLT: practice strict self-control] in all things. Now they *do it* to obtain a corruptible crown; but we an incorruptible." 1 Corinthians 9:25, KJV

In this passage, Paul is challenging the Corinthian believers to run the race of life in such a way as to earn the rewards of faithfulness. Again, Paul is not speaking about controlled drinking, but is, instead, teaching that controlled living is what leads to spiritual excellence. Therefore this passage cannot legitimately be used to condone moderate drinking.

- "For a bishop must be blameless, as the steward of God; not selfwilled, not soon angry, not given to wine, no striker, not given to filthy lucre; but a lover of hospitality, a lover of good men, sober, just, holy, temperate [NIV: disciplined & NLT: live a disciplined life];" Titus 1:7–8, KJV

This is one of the places in Scripture where Paul gives the requirements for the office of bishop/pastor. Before saying that a pastor should be temperate, Paul does say that the pastor should not be "given to wine," and of course, the advocates of drinking are quick to point this out. Was Paul suggesting that most pastors in the first century made a habit of drinking fermented wine? Was he saying that they could drink, just as long as they didn't get drunk? To find the answer, we must begin by asking: "If God forbade the priests in the Old Testament to drink fermented wines, why would he allow New Testament pastors to drink?" I believe He wouldn't!

To further emphasize this, Dr. William Patton wrote that the phrase "not given to wine" in the original Greek language literally means: " . . . not at, by, near, or with wine."[161] So the pastor was not only forbidden to use liquor, but was also forbidden to even be around the stuff. When Paul speaks of the pastor being temperate, he is teaching that a pastor should live a holy and disciplined life—not that he should learn how to "handle his liquor." I am confident that Titus 1 is not condoning moderate drinking—either in the life of the pastor or in the life of anyone else for that matter.

In addition, in the qualifications Paul gives for pastors in 1 Timothy 3:1–7, he says that the pastor should be vigilant (temperate in the NIV). This word is translated from the Greek word "*nephalios*" which literally means: "sober or to abstain from wine." So if Paul taught that pastors should abstain from wine in 1 Timothy 3, when he speaks of a pastor's temperance in Titus 1, isn't it reasonable to assume that he meant, in addition to general self-control, that a pastor should practice complete abstinence from wine? To be consistent, wouldn't the qualifications of the pastor Paul gave in Titus 1:7–8 be the same as those in 1 Timothy 3? Apparently, Timothy so interpreted Paul's message to mean that a pastor should abstain from fermented wines, that he was abstaining from all wines, both unfermented as well as fermented, and had to be encouraged by Paul to "drink a little wine" for his stomach problems.

- "That the aged men be sober, grave, temperate [NIV & NLT: self-controlled], sound in faith, in charity, in patience." Titus 2:2, KJV

Here Paul is encouraging the older men to be examples of godliness to the younger men in the church by living lives of self-control. Here Paul not only uses the word "temperate" but also uses the word "sober" which literally means "to abstain from wine." The word sober is often also used in the New Testament to refer to clearness and seriousness of mind. It could be argued that if Paul was referring to drinking, he gives a double command for abstinence by using both the word "temperate" and the word "sober." But, more than likely, what Paul intended to do was to encourage the older men to be sober-minded and to live controlled lives and wasn't even referring to drinking at all. Those who seek to find a concession for drinking alcohol in this passage are out of luck again.

• "Let your moderation [NIV: gentleness & NLT: see that you are considerate] be known unto all men. The Lord *is* at hand." Philippians 4:5, KJV

Many believers in favor of drinking say, "Okay, this is it! Here's where Paul says that a believer can drink as long as he drinks in moderation." Does he really say that? Does the word drinking or wine appear in this verse? Is there even the slightest suggestion in this passage that Paul was referring to moderate drinking? "No!"

In this passage, Paul is encouraging believers to live in such a way that their moderation (gentle and considerate ways) is obvious to everyone. He is stressing that the Christian life should be one of balance; believers should refrain from extremes of all kinds. He says that the possibility of the Lord's return at any moment should be a tremendous motivation for this. How strange that Paul would teach that having a reputation for being a moderate drinker would be a desirable thing to brag about to the Lord at His return. If those who believe that this passage is condoning moderate drinking are correct, then what about other indulgences? Wouldn't the same logic make it acceptable to include other questionable things as well? For example, wouldn't it then be acceptable for the believer to practice gluttony, lust, jealousy, gossiping, or laziness as long as he did so in moderation? If we can read drinking into this passage, can't we "read in" other things as well?

But if we can do this, it gives us the ability to make the Bible say just about anything we want it to say—especially when it concerns our "personal" sins and questionable habits. This is why we must be careful to never "read things into" a passage of Scripture, no matter how much we are tempted to do so. There is a warning in the book of Revelation concerning this:

> "And I solemnly declare to everyone who hears the prophetic words of this book: If anyone adds anything to what is written here, God will add to that person the plagues described in this book. And if anyone removes any of the words of this prophetic book, God will remove that person's share in the tree of life and in the holy city that are described in this book." Revelation 22:18–19, NLT

Even though this warning applies directly to the book of Revelation, most Bible scholars and teachers believe it also applies to the rest of Scripture as well.

Some ask, "But isn't Paul teaching in 1 Corinthians 10 that it is alright to drink alcohol as long as we drink it to God's glory?" Here's what this passage says:

> "If I can thank God for the food and enjoy it, why should I be condemned for eating it? Whatever you eat or drink or whatever you do, you must do all for the glory of God," 1 Corinthians 10:30–31, NLT

First, notice that alcohol is never mentioned. Here Paul is instructing believers to remember that in everything they do, they need to keep other believers in mind and should never do anything that would cause spiritual harm to them. Therefore, whether we are eating and drinking or doing something else, the welfare of others should be foremost in our minds. Paul says that it is actually possible to eat and drink to the benefit of others and to the glory of God at the same time. In spite of what some may want it to say, 1 Corinthians 10:30–31 does not specifically condone the use of alcohol.

Others ask, "Doesn't Paul tell us in Colossians 2 that we shouldn't allow anyone to condemn us for drinking alcohol?" Here's what Paul wrote to the Colossian believers:

> "So don't let anyone condemn you for what you eat or drink, or for not

celebrating certain holy days or new-moon ceremonies or Sabbaths."
Colossians 2:16, NLT

In this passage, Paul is explaining that born again believers no longer have to conform to the rigid requirements of Moses' Law. For example, those in Christ no longer need to observe holy days, new moon ceremonies, Sabbaths, or Jewish dietary rules. Since Jesus was the fulfillment of all things in God's law and obeyed them completely, in Christ, the believer too, satisfies the requirements of God's law. A person is not saved based upon what they eat and drink or refuse to eat and drink, but upon whether or not they have been born again. Therefore the Jews were wrong to insist that the new believers keep the ceremonial part of the law.

I think it is important to say at this point that a person's opinion about alcohol is not the litmus test that determines the genuineness of his salvation. Those who are convinced that drinking is wrong do not have the right to judge those who drink as unsaved. Although drinking is an important issue, it should not become a test of fellowship in the church. Given this, when Paul told the believers in Colossae not to allow anyone to condemn them for what they ate or drank, he was referring to the strict Jewish dietary rules found in Moses' law—he was not talking specifically about drinking alcohol.

Before we complete this part of our discussion, we need to consider one other passage that is often used as proof that the Bible encourages or allows the use of alcohol by believers. This passage is found in 1 Timothy 4:

"Now the Holy Spirit tells us clearly that in the last times some will turn away from what we believe; they will follow lying spirits and teachings that come from demons. These teachers are hypocrites and liars. They pretend to be religious, but their consciences are dead. They will say it is wrong to be married and wrong to eat certain foods. But God created those foods to be eaten with thanksgiving by people who know and believe the truth. Since everything God created is good, we should not reject any of it. We may receive it gladly, with thankful hearts. For we know it is made holy by the word of God and prayer."
1 Timothy 4:1–5, NLT

When those who condone the use of alcohol read this passage, they somehow find a justification for imbibing. Since Paul says that all things created by God are good, they naturally assume this also includes alcohol. It is true that unfermented wine (nothing more than fruit juice), which occurs naturally, is among the "foods" that God created and can be freely consumed with thanksgiving, but fermented wine is not. As we have already seen, fermentation that creates intoxicating wine for drinking is an unnatural process. Left alone to ferment, fruit juices spoil and become sour; they do not turn into desirable alcoholic beverages. It takes man's help for that. Since alcohol is a man-made substance, it cannot be included in "the things that God created." But more importantly, this passage isn't even referring to fermented wine. The primary subject of this passage is the demonic teachings of end-time false teachers, not believers drinking alcohol.

The literal message of this passage is that in the last days, false teachers "will follow lying spirits and teachings that come from demons." They will teach that salvation is based on outward works rather than an inward work of grace. Paul lists two of the distinguishing characteristics of these demonic doctrines:

- Aberrant beliefs about marriage.
- The belief that godliness is produced by physical rather than spiritual disciplines.

John MacArthur points out:

> "Anything contrary to Scripture can be the entry point of demonic teaching. We might have expected the apostle to follow his severe comments about demon doctrine with examples like denying the Trinity or the deity of the Savior, or rejecting salvation by grace. But Satan is so subtle and seeks to gain a foothold on territory more easily yielded. Paul gives a sample of what was being taught at Ephesus. The deceivers were focusing on two seemingly minor teachings: that spirituality demanded avoiding marriage and abstaining from foods. As is typical of satanic deception, both of those teachings contain an element of spiritual service . . . The deception comes in seeing those as essential

elements of salvation. The devising of human means of salvation is a hallmark of all false religion . . . The emphasis on externalism that marked the Ephesian apostates is typical of all satanic false religion. From the animism of primitive tribes to the sophistication of major world religions, men rely on good works, outward ritual, and self denial . . . Believers are complete in Christ and do not need to practice physical self-denial to gain salvation from sin and righteousness before God."[162]

Concerning this passage, William Barclay, the great theologian wrote:

"This was an ever-recurring heresy in the Church; in every generation men arose who tried to be stricter than God."[163]

In other words, salvation is found by trusting in Christ and His finished work on the cross, not by our own works, asceticism, or anything else. We must not add to, or take away from the Gospel. The first chapter of Galatians warns:

"Let God's curse fall on anyone, including myself, who preaches any other message than the one we told you about. Even if an angel comes from heaven and preaches any other message, let him be forever cursed. I will say it again: If anyone preaches any other gospel than the one you welcomed, let God's curse fall upon that person." Galatians 1:8–9, NLT

The message of salvation by grace, through faith, is the one, true Gospel and any other is a counterfeit.

The verdict is clear: the case cannot be made, using this passage or any other, that Paul was encouraging the use of alcohol among believers. Once again, this illustrates the reason we must use the utmost care when interpreting the Scriptures. If we don't, we run the real risk of making a huge interpretational error, effectively making mincemeat out of the Scriptures. If 1 Timothy 4:1–5 is interpreted to teach that anything is good for consumption (specifically alcohol), imagine the implications! If this interpretation is correct, then not only would alcohol be permissible for believers, but wouldn't other harmful drugs be permissible as well? Can you imagine God encouraging believers to use LSD, cocaine, or heroine? Ridiculous you say? Not really. Alcohol is as much a drug as is LSD, cocaine, or heroine. Since this passage isn't even talking about alcohol in the first place, we would be as justified to include LSD as we would to include alcohol. If we can "read in" alcohol, we can "read in" other things as well! By following the principles of hermeneutics and plain old common sense, we can avoid making such foolish mistakes.

A LITTLE SNORT FOR PREACHERS AND DEACONS?

When giving the qualifications for pastors and deacons, Paul wrote:

> "Here is a trustworthy saying: If anyone sets his heart on being an overseer [pastor], he desires a noble task. Now the overseer must be above reproach, the husband of but one wife, temperate, self-controlled, respectable, hospitable, able to teach, not given to drunkenness, not violent but gentle, not quarrelsome, not a lover of money." 1 Timothy 3:1–3, NIV

> "Deacons, likewise, are to be men worthy of respect, sincere, not indulging in much wine, and not pursuing dishonest gain. They must keep hold of the deep truths of the faith with a clear conscience. They must first be tested; and then if there is nothing against them, let them serve as deacons." 1 Timothy 3:8–10, NIV

Do the phrases: "not given to drunkenness" and "not indulging in much wine" in these passages give preachers and deacons the right to take a "little snort" from time to time? Those who seek a biblical concession for drinking alcohol say yes. I say no!

First, we must notice that Paul wrote that pastors and deacons must be men of high moral character—men above reproach. To be above reproach involves more than avoiding alcohol—it involves "abstaining from all appearance of evil" (1 Thessalonians 5:22, KJV) or as the New International Version translates it:

"avoiding every kind of evil." Now if the wine Paul was speaking of was unfermented, this passage poses no problem for us. What creates a problem is if Paul was referring to fermented wine. To be consistent, shouldn't those who argue that Paul believed pastors and deacons could drink "some" fermented wine also believe that pastors and deacons could practice other sinful activities as long as they didn't make a habit of it? For instance, couldn't they: quarrel "some," give in to "some" greed, practice "some" gluttony and still be qualified to lead Christ's church? Sound ludicrous? That's because it is.

From what we have learned about alcohol, insisting that pastors and deacons have the right to drink "some" fermented wine undermines everything Scripture teaches about alcohol. As has already been stated, if God wouldn't allow the priests to drink, why would He allow pastors and deacons to drink? Remember that, as we discussed earlier, one of the qualifications Paul gives for pastors and deacons as well, is that they be sober (translated "temperate" in the NIV). Again, the Greek word for "sober/temperate" is *nephalios* which means to abstain from wine. Therefore, it appears that Paul believed that preachers and deacons should be teetotalers.

In addition, I am convinced that Paul was saying that, since the wines of his day were weak often requiring the consumption of large quantities to cause intoxication, the deacons were not to consume much wine (Remember: Not all references to wine in the Bible refer to fermented wine—the wines of their day were often so weak, they wouldn't even compare with our strong wines today). To make the quantum leap and compare their wines to our wines is like comparing apples to oranges. For example, today a pastor/deacon needs no warning to avoid drinking large amounts of modern wines, which are much more intoxicating than those of Bible times, because he knows that only a little alcohol can cause intoxication. This was not the case in Paul's day. Therefore Paul was instructing deacons to avoid even the "appearance of drunkenness" by only drinking small amounts of "weak" wine to protect their reputations.

Some point out Paul's advice to Timothy in 1 Timothy 5:23 as a concession for drinking alcohol. As we saw previously, Paul encouraged Timothy to drink a little wine because he was having stomach problems. It is important for us to remember that apparently Timothy believed so strongly that Christians (pastors in particular) should not consume fermented wines that he abstained from all wines—even those that were unfermented. Therefore, Paul had to urge Timothy to drink a little wine to help ease his chronic stomach problems. It seems reasonable to assume (especially after learning what the Bible really teaches about alcohol) that Paul would have intended for Timothy to drink unfermented wine. Regardless of whether the wine was fermented or unfermented, it is clear that Paul was encouraging the use of wine for medicinal purposes only. This same medicinal reason for drinking alcohol is also given in the Old Testament:

> "Liquor is for the dying, and wine for those in deep depression. Let them drink to forget their poverty and remember their troubles no more." Proverbs 31:6–7, NLT

Dr. Ed Rickard says that this passage was intended to give permission for those going through sudden trauma to use some alcohol to help them cope with the immediate shock:

> "The occasion for wine should not be misunderstood. The passage is not talking about a sorrow linked to either a recurring depression or a chronic state of poverty, for drinking aggravates both conditions. Rather, it is talking about a grief caused by sudden overwhelming loss, either of loved ones or possessions. Today a victim of such loss might be given a sedative. Yet a believer need not rely on the help of drugs to endure great sorrow. Following David's example when the Amalekites stole his family and wealth, [believers] can encourage [themselves] in the Lord (1 Sam. 30:6)."[164]

The ancients of Bible times believed that wine had healing qualities; therefore, they often used it in the same way that we use medicines today. This is the reason wine is mentioned in the parable of the "Good Samaritan":

"But a Samaritan, as he traveled, came where the man was; and when he saw him, he took pity on him. He went to him and bandaged his wounds, pouring on oil and wine." Luke 10:33–34, NIV

In fact, even some of our modern medicines contain moderate amounts of alcohol.

Some often attempt to condone their drinking by quoting physicians who claim that a small glass of wine each day is good for the body—especially the heart. Even if this is true, this would provide no excuse for social drinking. In the article, "Alcohol, Wine, and Cardiovascular Disease," the American Heart Association declares:

"Over the past several decades, many studies have been published in science journals about how drinking alcohol may be associated with reduced mortality due to heart disease in some populations. Some researchers have suggested that the benefit may be due to wine, especially red wine. Others are examining the potential benefits of components in red wine such as flavonoids (FLAV'oh-noidz) and other antioxidants (an"tih-OK'sih-dants) in reducing heart disease risk. Some of these components may be found in other foods such as grapes or red grape juice. **The linkage reported in many of these studies may be due to other lifestyle factors rather than alcohol. Such factors may include increased physical activity, and a diet high in fruits and vegetables and lower in saturated fats.** No direct comparison trials have been done to determine the specific effect of wine or other alcohol on the risk of developing heart disease or stroke."[165]

Notice, some of the components in red wine that promote health can also be found in grapes or red grape juice. They also admit that the wine may not have as much to do with improving health as do lifestyle factors such as physical activity and a healthy diet. It is also important to note that other equally qualified professionals and physicians have stated that drinking a glass of pure grape juice each day will have the same positive effect as drinking a glass of fermented wine. Gloria Tsang, R.D. says:

"**Grapes, many other fruits and vegetables, and regular physical activities offer the same benefits for the heart as seen in alcohol.** Include a variety of fruits and vegetables in your diet to maximize the heart health benefits . . . Should I start drinking more red wine now? The answer is No. Studies showed that alcohol drinking may increase triglycerides . . . and result in weight gain due to its empty calories. Other studies also suggested that alcohol consumption is associated with cancer risk . . . The American Heart Association cautions people NOT to start drinking if they do not already drink alcohol."[166]

The Yale-New Haven Hospital in New Haven, Connecticut warns:

"Recommendations to consume moderate amounts of wine are limited to individuals with a clean bill of health. It is clear that people with medical and social conditions worsened by alcohol should not consume any alcohol at all . . . In 1997, researchers at the University of Wisconsin concluded that purple grape juice also reduced blood clotting. Another study by researchers at the University of California at Davis, confirmed the findings that **non-alcoholic red wine [grape juice] contains the same antioxidant profile as red wine.**"[167]

So, regardless of what kind of wine Paul was encouraging Timothy to use, we can be certain that he was not giving Timothy the permission to gather together a group of believers and throw a New Testament "kegger!"

Charles Wesley Ewing made some interesting observations about Timothy's situation:

"Timothy was a native of the city of Lystra in Lycaonia. At the time of Paul's letter to him, Timothy was at Ephesus. Both of the places are in Asia Minor. The water in that region was strongly alkali and was upsetting to Timothy's stomach. Paul was giving him advice on how to get rid of his stomach disorder. It was the practice in those days, and it is still practiced today in Syria, Mesopotamia, and other parts of Asia Minor, that when people drank this alkali water they would mix it with a spoon full of jam made from boiling the juice of grapes that are similar to our own Concord grape. The acids in the grape jam would neutralize the alkali in the water and make it fit for the stomach. This is what Paul was telling Timothy to do."[168]

Roger Campbell and Dr. Jack Van Impe summed it up pretty well when they stated:

"We can be certain that Paul would not have compromised the unity of the Scriptures in order to provide a few cups of wine for thirsty deacons in the early church."[169]

Chapter 10

WILL DRINKING SEND ME TO HELL?

To some, this is all that seems to matter. Apparently they feel that as long as a particular sin won't cause them to go to Hell, it's worth risking their spiritual welfare to go ahead and commit it. Now I must admit that when compared to where a person will spend eternity, everything else, such as drinking and drunkenness, does pale in comparison. But for the follower of Christ, is getting to Heaven all that really matters? Is simply making it through the "pearly gates" the ultimate goal of Christianity? The book of Hebrews says otherwise:

> "So let us stop going over the basics of Christianity again and again. Let us go on instead and become mature in our understanding. Surely we don't need to start all over again with the importance of turning away from evil deeds and placing our faith in God. You don't need further instruction about baptisms, the laying on of hands, the resurrection of the dead, and eternal judgment. And so, God willing, we will move forward to further understanding." Hebrews 6:1–3, NLT

In other words, it's important that believers "nail down" their salvation so they can move on to spiritual maturity. God's goal is not just to get "baby" believers safely into Heaven; His ultimate goal is to develop mature believers who, as they become more and more like Jesus, can make an eternal difference in the lives of others. The New Testament is filled with challenges for the believer's spiritual growth:

> "You must crave pure spiritual milk so that you can grow into the fullness of your salvation. Cry out for this nourishment as a baby cries for milk," 1 Peter 2:2, NLT

"But grow in grace, and in the knowledge of our Lord and Saviour Jesus Christ . . ." 2 Peter 3:18, KJV

"I don't mean to say that I have already achieved these things or that I have already reached perfection! But I keep working toward that day when I will finally be all that Christ Jesus saved me for and wants me to be. No, dear brothers and sisters, I am still not all I should be, but I am focusing all my energies on this one thing: Forgetting the past and looking forward to what lies ahead, I strain to reach the end of the race and receive the prize for which God, through Christ Jesus, is calling us up to heaven. I hope all of you who are mature Christians will agree on these things." Philippians 3:12–15, NLT

Spiritual growth becomes even more important when we realize that all believers must give an account to God for the lives they have lived. Although the Bible emphatically teaches that salvation is a gift (Romans 6:23) that cannot be earned or deserved (Ephesians 2:8–9), it also clearly teaches that Jesus saves us to live godly lives that produce good works (Ephesians 2:10). At the Judgment Seat of Christ, our lives will be evaluated. Paul discussed this judgment of believers in 2 Corinthians:

"For we must all appear before the judgment seat of Christ, that each one may receive what is due him for the things done while in the body, whether good or bad." 2 Corinthians 5:10, NIV

In 1 Corinthians 3, Paul emphasized that the primary purpose of this judgment is to determine the rewards believers have earned by faithful living:

" . . . his work will be shown for what it is, because the Day will bring it to light. It will be revealed with fire, and the fire will test the quality of each man's work. If what he has built survives, he will receive his reward. If it is burned up, he will suffer loss; he himself will be saved, but only as one escaping through the flames." 1 Corinthians 3:13–15, NIV

Notice that, regardless of the rewards a believer has or has not earned, his salvation is not in doubt. Those who have not committed themselves to faithful living will "suffer loss" but will still be saved, but only as those "escaping through the flames." Although true believers are secure in their salvation, they will face serious consequences for disobedience. So instead of wondering if drinking will cause them to end up in Hell (because it won't), the believer should be asking himself if drinking will damage his spiritual growth and cause him to suffer loss at the Judgment Seat of Christ.

But what about unbelievers; will drinking alcohol send them to Hell? The answer is both yes and no.

DO PEOPLE GO TO HELL BECAUSE THEY SIN?

A common misconception is that people go to Hell because they sin. The truth is people sin because they are born going to Hell. Sadly, every person is born separated from God and on his way to a lost eternity. In the beginning, this was not so. When the first man, Adam, was created, he was made in the image of God and was free from sin (Gen 1:26–27). But when Adam sinned in the Garden of Eden, his nature changed into one that made him prone to sin and that separated him from God. The Bible calls this separation spiritual death. When Adam and Eve had children, rather than being made in God's image as Adam had been, they were born in Adam's image and inherited his sinful nature. This is easily seen in Genesis 5:

> "When Adam had lived 130 years, he had a son in his own likeness, in his own image; and he named him Seth." Genesis 5:3, NIV

Each successive generation has received this sinful nature and has started life on the road to Hell. In the book of Romans we read:

> "Therefore, just as sin entered the world through one man, and death [physical & spiritual] through sin, and in this way death came to all men, because all sinned . . ." Romans 5:12, NIV

> "There is no one righteous, not even one . . . for all have sinned and fall short of the glory of God," Romans 3:10, 23, NIV

"For the wages of sin is death [physical & spiritual] . . ." Romans 6:23, NIV

According to Jesus, every person falls into one of two categories: those who are with Him and those who are against Him—there is no middle ground:

"He who is not with me is against me, and he who does not gather with me scatters." Matthew 12:30, NIV

Unfortunately, because of the sinful nature we inherit from Adam, we are all born turned "against" Jesus, and in spite of what we may have heard or may want to believe, we are not God's children by our original birth. Although this is not good news, the Bible also has some good news for us: God did not leave us in this deplorable state. He made a way for us to become part of His family by the process of a new birth, a spiritual birth that transforms us into a new creation that allows us to be "with" instead of "against" Him:

"Jesus replied, 'I assure you, unless you are **born again**, you can never see the Kingdom of God.' 'What do you mean?' exclaimed Nicodemus. 'How can an old man go back into his mother's womb and be born again?' Jesus replied, 'The truth is, no one can enter the Kingdom of God without being born of water and the Spirit. Humans can reproduce only human life, but the Holy Spirit gives new life from heaven. So don't be surprised at my statement that you must be **born again**.'" John 3:3–7, NLT

"Therefore, if anyone is in Christ, he is a new creation; the old has gone, the new has come!" 2 Corinthians 5:17, NIV

When this new birth occurs, we who were born outside of God's family originally, are brought into God's forever family by the process of adoption:

"But to all who believed him and accepted him, he gave the right to **become children of God**. They are **reborn**! This is not a physical birth resulting from human passion or plan—this rebirth comes from God." John 1:12, 13, NLT

"So you should not be like cowering, fearful slaves. You should behave Instead like God's very own children, **adopted** into his family—calling him 'Father, dear Father.' For his Holy Spirit speaks to us deep in our hearts and tells us that we are God's children. And since we are his children, we will share his treasures—for everything God gives to his Son, Christ, is ours, too." Romans 8:15–17, NLT

This is why the Bible calls this message the Gospel which literally means "good news":

"Day after day, in the temple courts and from house to house, they never stopped teaching and proclaiming the good news that Jesus is the Christ." Acts 5:42, NIV

"I am not ashamed of the gospel, because it is the power of God for the salvation of everyone who believes: first for the Jew, then for the Gentile." Romans 1:16, NIV

"And you also were included in Christ when you heard the word of truth, the gospel of your salvation." Ephesians 1:13, NIV

By trusting in Christ and what He did for us through His death on the cross and His resurrection, we cease to be Adam's sons dominated by Adam's sins, and we become God's sons receiving His righteousness (2 Cor. 5:21).

Therefore, in the final analysis, it is not sin that sends us to Hell, but the source of that sin—a sinful nature. Drinking, drunkenness, and other sinful acts are only evidences of a deeper problem. Sins alone are not the ultimate reason why some will be lost forever. Rejecting Christ as their personal Lord and Savior, thereby cutting off all hope of salvation, is what will cause them to eventually end up in Hell.

But even though all of this is true, the Bible still clearly declares that drunkards will not be in Heaven. Why is this?

DRINK, DRANK, DRUNK

For some reason, when we think of really wicked sins we think of murder, thievery, sexual perversion, etc., but seldom do we think of drunkenness. With slurred speech, clumsy actions, and funny wit, drunks are often portrayed as likeable, loveable teddy bears that wouldn't harm a flea. Characters like Otis on *The Andy Griffith Show* and the drunken millionaire played by Dudley Moore in the movie *Arthur* immediately come to mind. It's odd that we find such humor in drunkenness because God does not. As I have already stated, drunkenness normally serves as a door for all other perversions (Prov. 23:29–35) and that's why the Scriptures condemn it so sternly. Here's how God views it:

" . . . So let us put aside the deeds of darkness and put on the armor of light. Let us behave decently, as in the daytime, not in orgies and **drunkenness**, not in sexual immorality and debauchery, not in dissension and jealousy." Romans 13:12–13, NIV

"What I meant was that you are not to associate with anyone who claims to be a Christian yet indulges in sexual sin, or is greedy, or worships idols, or is abusive, or a **drunkard**, or a swindler. Don't even eat with such people." 1 Corinthians 5:11, NLT

"Don't you know that those who do wrong will have no share in the Kingdom of God? Don't fool yourselves. Those who indulge in sexual sin, who are idol worshipers, adulterers, male prostitutes, homosexuals, thieves, greedy people, **drunkards**, abusers, and swindlers—none of these will have a share in the Kingdom of God." 1 Corinthians 6:9–10, NLT

"The acts of the sinful nature are obvious: sexual immorality, impurity and debauchery; idolatry and witchcraft; hatred, discord, jealousy, fits of rage, selfish ambition, dissensions, factions and envy; **drunkenness**, orgies, and the like. I warn you, as I did before, that those who live like this will not inherit the kingdom of God." Galatians 5:19–21, NIV

Although drunkenness will not be the reason people go to Hell, not one drunkard will be in Heaven. You may know someone who claims to be a Christian but has a habit of overindulging in drinking or in some other sinful practice. Notice carefully that in 1 Corinthians 5:11, Paul says that people who practice sins such as drunkenness may claim to be believers, but in reality are probably not and should be disassociated from the fellowship of the believers.

Although it is feasible that a believer could, in a moment of weakness, drink too much and get drunk, I believe the Scriptures teach that there is good reason to question the salvation of anyone who habitually gets drunk. This is why, in 2 Corinthians, Paul encouraged everyone to examine the genuineness of their salvation:

> "Examine yourselves to see if your faith is really genuine. Test yourselves. If you cannot tell that Jesus Christ is among you, it means you have failed the test." 2 Corinthians 13:5

For the true believer, salvation always produces evidence. The books of James and 1 John emphasize this. In the life of the false believer there will be no such evidence—professing salvation is not the same as possessing it:

> "Dear brothers and sisters, what's the use of saying you have faith if you don't prove it by your actions? That kind of faith can't save anyone . . . So you see, it isn't enough just to have faith. Faith that doesn't show itself by good deeds is no faith at all—it is dead and useless. Now someone may argue, 'Some people have faith; others have good deeds.' I say, 'I can't see your faith if you don't have good deeds, but I will show you my faith through my good deeds.' Do you still think it's enough just to believe that there is one God? Well, even the demons believe this, and they tremble in terror! Fool! When will you ever learn that faith that does not result in good deeds is useless?" James 2:13, 17–20, NLT

> "If someone says, 'I belong to God,' but doesn't obey God's commandments, that person is a liar and does not live in the truth. But those who obey God's word really do love him. That is the way to know whether or not we live in him. Those who say they live in God should live their lives as Christ did." 1 John 2:4–6, NLT

The clear teaching of Scripture is that all sins can be forgiven, but once a person becomes a believer, he does not live the same thereafter—i.e. those who were liars stop lying, those who stole stop stealing, and those who were drunkards stop drinking. In 1 Corinthians 6, Paul says that some of the believers at Corinth had been drunkards before coming to Christ, but after their conversion they had ceased living a drunkard's life:

"Don't you know that those who do wrong will have no share in the Kingdom of God? Don't fool yourselves. Those who indulge in sexual sin, who are idol worshipers, adulterers, male prostitutes, homosexuals, thieves, greedy people, **drunkards**, abusers, and swindlers—none of these will have a share in the Kingdom of God. There was a time when some of you were just like that, but now your sins have been washed away, and you have been set apart for God. You have been made right with God because of what the Lord Jesus Christ and the Spirit of our God have done for you." 1 Corinthians 6:9–11, NLT

Certainly, the church must be patient with those who have recently come to Christ. Often these new believers have been saved from lives dominated by sinful habits. The job of the church is to disciple these new converts, assisting them in gaining victory over the control of such ingrained sins. The last thing these new believers need is condemnation from impatient or judgmental, self-righteous believers. The church must find the delicate balance between being patient with new, developing believers and being overly tolerant of sinful lifestyles.

Some argue that there is a difference between drinking and getting drunk. They say, "So what's the big deal with a believer drinking as long as they don't get drunk?" I realize that drinking is not the same as being drunk and that some people can drink without getting drunk, but for the life of me, I can't understand why believers would willingly indulge in something like drinking, a practice characteristic of millions who will spend eternity in Hell. In addition, since we have no way of knowing who has the potential of becoming a bona fide alcoholic, why would anyone roll the dice by drinking? I've known alcoholics who would give anything if they could just take back that first drink. One thing is certain: a person has to drink to get drunk. The best prevention for drunkenness is simply not to drink in the first place.

One other thing might need to be said about drunkenness. As we know, some seem to be born with a genetic tendency for drunkenness. Alcoholism is a terrible sickness that destroys millions of lives. What is of concern is the tendency of our society to label almost everything the Bible calls a sin as an illness instead. Admittedly, some seem to have a weakness for addictions and should seek help from qualified professionals, but I fear much sin is simply excused as a disease. Dr. Ed Rickard writes:

> "A few scientific studies suggest that some people have a natural predisposition to alcoholism, as a result of quirks in their brain chemistry favoring dependence upon alcohol as the only means of sustaining a sense of well being. Such studies do not, however, support the idea that alcoholism is simply a disease. A man may be powerless to resist a disease, but though he has a predisposition to alcoholism, he need not become an alcoholic. He can resist it and escape it altogether by exercising his freedom of will. A predisposition to alcoholism, if it exists, is nothing but a weakness for the sin of drunkenness, like the weaknesses some people have for the sins of lust or anger. Everyone has points of special vulnerability to the darts of temptation."[170]

So, even though a believer will not go to Hell for drinking, there remains an issue that drinking believers must grapple with: Are they willing, by their drinking, to become the reason why others may go there? Is drinking worth that much to them?

Chapter 11

ONE MAN'S FREEDOM IS ANOTHER MAN'S BONDAGE

I can almost hear those in favor of drinking screaming: "But what about my freedom in Christ? Didn't Jesus say that if He sets someone free, they're totally free? Doesn't the Bible say that where the Spirit of the Lord is there is liberty? Why should my liberty be limited by someone else's lack of maturity, tolerance, or understanding?"

First of all, without question, the Bible emphatically teaches that Jesus does indeed set the believer free. But is this freedom intended to give believers the right to do whatever they want— even if it hurts other believers and unbelievers as well? Of course not, but those who drink always seem to have a way of justifying their drinking. Their arguments go something like this:

- We're mature adults, we don't intend to hurt anyone so what's the problem? If people are offended by our drinking, that's their problem.
- We're celebrating a special occasion and we want to drink wine with our meal. How's that going to hurt anyone?
- I'm hot and thirsty. What's wrong with having a cold beer?
- We're on vacation and no one here even knows us, so who's it going to hurt if we have a drink?

Honestly, does any believer really think that drinking isn't going to damage his testimony and the conscience of those who see it—especially unbelievers who know him? What do you imagine is the first thing that the average person thinks when he sees a believer drinking alcohol?

For example, let's say that as a believer, I only drink two or three beers a year. Imagine that I've just finished mowing the yard, I'm thirsty, and I decide to drink one of those beers. Let's say that you're a new believer that I've recently helped lead to Christ and as an unbeliever you drank for years. Now that you're a believer, you feel you should stop drinking. On this particular day, you make an unannounced visit and "catch me" in the backyard drinking my beer. What do you think will be your first thought? Or let's imagine that you've never come to Christ because of the hypocrites you've seen in the church. Recently, I've been reaching out to you and you're on the verge of making a commitment to Christ. Now, let's say that you make that unannounced visit and catch me in my backyard drinking one of the few beers I'll drink all year. Do you think that will have any negative impact on your faith in me and your decision about becoming a believer? Of course it will!

Believe me, after over twenty years of being a pastor the first thing most people think when they see a believer drinking alcohol is: HYPOCRITE! This may not be fair, but given alcohol's reputation, what else should they think? Regardless of whether or not the drinking believer intends to get drunk, others looking on (especially unbelievers) don't know that and are confused. For years, the number one excuse I've heard people give for not becoming a Christian is the hypocrites they've seen in the church. Honestly, I have to agree. I too have seen far too many believers (only God knows if they were real or fake) who lived such careless lives that they made Christianity look more like a joke than a genuine relationship with God. Do you honestly believe Christ gave us spiritual freedom so we could live lives that cause such confusion in the minds of those around us?

Although we saw in the last chapter that drinking won't send a believer to Hell, I think it is important to emphasize that a drinking believer may create just enough doubt or distaste in the mind of an unbeliever that he will write off Christianity as a bunch of religious "mumbo jumbo", reject Christ, and end up going to Hell himself. Even though this may sound a little harsh, I'm convinced that hypocritical, careless Christians do incredible damage to the cause of Christ and influence thousands to remain unsaved. Since **64% of Protestants drink**[171] and since drinking believers are seen by many (I believe by most) as hypocrites, I believe drinking believers will be the reason millions end up in Hell someday.

Before I am labeled as a legalist, let me say that one of the most exciting truths taught in Scripture is that Christ liberates those who trust in Him:

> "Jesus said to the people who believed in him, 'You are truly my disciples if you keep obeying my teachings. And you will know the truth, and the truth will set you free . . . So if the Son sets you free, you will indeed be free.'" John 8:32, 36, NLT

> "Now the Lord is the Spirit, and where the Spirit of the Lord is, there is freedom." 2 Corinthians 3:17, NIV

All who have been born again know this freedom—a freedom of the soul—a freedom like no other, found only in Christ. No longer do we have to earn God's acceptance by keeping a long list of do's and don'ts; we are accepted because of His grace. The heavy yoke of legalism is lifted from the shoulders of all who are "in Christ." Jesus even said:

> "Come to me, all of you who are weary and carry heavy burdens, and I will give you rest. Take my yoke upon you. Let me teach you, because I am humble and gentle, and you will find rest for your souls. For my yoke fits perfectly, and the burden I give you is light." Matthew 11:28–30, NLT

> "It is for freedom that Christ has set us free. Stand firm, then, and do not let yourselves be burdened again by a yoke of slavery." Galatians 5:1, NIV

But does Jesus liberate believers so they can participate in questionable, self-indulgent activities (such as drinking) no matter how harmful they may be to themselves and others?

BELIEVERS WILL NEVER BE OUT OF DEBT!

Because salvation is a gift, believers owe a huge debt—a debt toward God and a debt toward others. A full appreciation of this debt makes a big impact in the way a believer views his freedom in Christ. Motivated by his deep sense of indebtedness, Paul confessed:

> "For I have a great sense of obligation to people in our culture and to people in other cultures, to the educated and uneducated alike." Romans 1:14, NLT

It was this indebtedness that drove him to reach beyond himself to minister to others:

> "Though I am free and belong to no man, I make myself a slave to everyone, to win as many as possible. To the Jews I became like a Jew, to win the Jews. To those under the law I became like one under the law (though I myself am not under the law), so as to win those under the law. To those not having the law I became like one not having the law (though I am not free from God's law but am under Christ's law), so as to win those not having the law. To the weak I became weak, to win the weak. I have become all things to all men so that by all possible means I might save some. I do all this for the sake of the gospel, that I may share in its blessings." 1 Corinthians 9:19–23, NIV

This is why, when he wrote to the believers at Philippi, Paul urged them to remember that their Christian liberty must be tempered by a deep concern for the welfare of others:

> "Do nothing out of selfish ambition or vain conceit, but in humility consider others better than yourselves. Each of you should look not only to your own interests, but also to the interests of others. Your attitude should be the same as that of Christ Jesus:" Philippians 2:3–5, NIV

In short, Paul was saying that believers cannot operate under the illusion that life is all about them. This self-centered brand of Christianity, the antithesis of everything Jesus taught, causes us to lose sight of our primary mission on earth: to honor God and reach others for Him. John R. W. Stott wrote:

"The reason these [Paul's] affirmations are so striking is that they are in direct antithesis to the attitude of many in the contemporary church. People nowadays tend to regard evangelism as an optional extra and consider (if they engage in it) that they are conferring a favour on God; Paul spoke of it as an obligation. The modern mood is one of reluctance; Paul's was one of eagerness or enthusiasm . . . Similarly, we are debtors to the world, even though we are not apostles. If the gospel has come to us (which it has), we have no liberty to keep it to ourselves . . . Such was Paul's first incentive. He was eager because he was in debt. It is universally regarded as a dishonourable thing to leave a debt unpaid. We should be as eager to discharge our debt as Paul was to discharge his.[172]

Jesus emphasized this when He spoke of the two great commandments:

"One of them, an expert in religious law, tried to trap him with this question: 'Teacher, which is the most important commandment in the law of Moses?' Jesus replied, 'You must love the Lord your God with all your heart, all your soul, and all your mind. This is the first and greatest commandment. A second is equally important: Love your neighbor as yourself. All the other commandments and all the demands of the prophets are based on these two commandments.'" Matthew 22:35–40, NLT

According to Jesus, the essence of Christian living can be defined with two principles:

1. Being more interested in God than in anything else.
2. Being more interested in others than self.

As we struggle with issues like drinking, these two principles are indispensable guidelines. As we enjoy our Christian liberty, the effect our actions have on others should always weigh heavily on our hearts and minds.

WHAT DID JESUS DIE TO FREE US FROM?

Jesus: left His throne in heaven, became a man, lived a

perfect life, faced down the Devil, tolerated the ridicule of the religious world, reached out in compassion to the sick and down-trodden, allowed the mockery of his so-called trial, took the cruel beating and torture, endured the cross, received the wrath of God on mankind's behalf, died, came back from the dead, and ascended to heaven to intercede for believers. Did He do all of this just so believers could satisfy their selfish appetites? Certainly not! So "from what" and "for what" did He free us?

First of all, Paul wrote in his letter to the Christians in Rome that Jesus freed us from the power of sin:

> "For the power of the life-giving Spirit has freed you through Christ Jesus from the power of sin that leads to death." Romans 8:2, NLT

As we saw in chapter nine, we can thank Adam for the sinful nature that produces spiritual death in all of us. But thankfully, the last Adam (Jesus) took away what the first Adam gave to us:

> "For this one man, Adam, brought death to many through his sin. But this other man, Jesus Christ, brought forgiveness to many through God's bountiful gift. The sin of this one man, Adam, caused death to rule over us, but all who receive God's wonderful, gracious gift of righteousness will live in triumph over sin and death through this one man, Jesus Christ." Romans 5:15, 17, NLT

> "The Scriptures tell us, 'The first man, Adam, became a living person.' But the last Adam—that is, Christ—is a life-giving Spirit." 1 Corinthians 15:45, NLT

So in Jesus (the last Adam), believers are freed from both the penalty of sin and the burdensome yoke of the Old Testament Law (that no man could satisfy):

> "He forgave us all our sins, having canceled the written code [O.T. Law], with its regulations, that was against us and that stood opposed to us; he took it away, nailing it to the cross. And having disarmed the powers and authorities, he made a public spectacle of them, triumphing over them by the cross." Colossians 2:13–15, NIV

Having been set free from the Law, Peter warned believers

to never allow themselves or any other believer to again be placed back under the burden of the law:

> "Why are you now questioning God's way by burdening the Gentile believers with a yoke [Moses' Law] that neither we nor our ancestors were able to bear? We believe that we are all saved the same way, by the special favor of the Lord Jesus." Acts 15:10–11, NLT

Paul gave this same warning to the believers in Galatia:

> "So Christ has really set us free. Now make sure that you stay free, and don't get tied up again in slavery to the law." Galatians 5:1, NLT

> "Even that question wouldn't have come up except for some so-called Christians there—false ones, really—who came to spy on us and see our freedom in Christ Jesus. They wanted to force us, like slaves, to follow their Jewish regulations. But we refused to listen to them for a single moment. We wanted to preserve the truth of the Good News for you." Galatians 2:4–5, NLT

It is evident that the Scriptures teach that Jesus came to free us from the Law, its curse, and the bondage of sin—but He never intended to free us from all obligations. Although free from Moses' Law, the believer is still obligated to the Law of Christ (principles found in the New Testament that produce a lifestyle honoring to Jesus):

> "So since God's grace has set us free from the law, does this mean we can go on sinning? Of course not! Don't you realize that whatever you choose to obey becomes your master?" Romans 6:15–16, NLT

> "When I am with the Gentiles who do not have the Jewish law, I fit in with them as much as I can. In this way, I gain their confidence and bring them to Christ. But I do not discard the law of God; I obey the **law of Christ**." 1 Corinthians 9:21, NLT

> "Carry each other's burdens, and in this way you will fulfill the **law of Christ**." Galatians 6:2, NIV

Rather than being a license for us to indulge in sinful practices, our freedom in Christ should be an incentive to live a Christ-like life—thus fulfilling the Law of Christ.

FREEDOM HAS ITS LIMITS

Freedom ceases to be freedom if it produces bondage. When indulging in questionable activities like drinking, though some may sincerely believe they are simply exercising their liberty in Christ, they should ask themselves: "Does this activity liberate or enslave?" This is what the Apostle Peter was referring to when he spoke of how the false teachers in his day were attempting to engage new believers in activities that would once again entangle them in the bondage of sin:

> "With lustful desire as their bait, they lure back into sin those who have just escaped from such wicked living. They promise freedom, but they themselves are slaves to sin and corruption. For you are a slave to whatever controls you." 2 Peter 2:18–19, NLT

He warned the first century believers that they would become the slaves of whatever sin they allowed to control them, and the same warning is apropos for believers today.

But many do not believe that drinking is sinful and are convinced that it is a permissible practice for a believer. Even if this is true (though the facts prove otherwise), Paul taught that though something might be permissible for a believer, it may not be spiritually profitable:

> "Everything is permissible for me—but not everything is beneficial. Everything is permissible for me—but I will not be mastered by anything." 1 Corinthians 6:12, NIV

Stated simply—the believer's freedom has limits. When a believer uses liberty as an excuse to commit sinful acts, he has gone beyond what Scripture means when it speaks of Christian liberty:

> "For you have been called to live in freedom—not freedom to satisfy your sinful nature, but freedom to serve one another in love." Galatians 5:13, NLT

In this passage, Paul used Greek words which were actually military terms. Their literal meaning is: believers should never use their liberty as a "headquarters from which to launch sinful campaigns." Peter concurs by saying:

> "Live as free men, but do not use your freedom as a cover-up for evil; live as servants of God." 1 Peter 2:16, NIV

It is sad that so many believers use God's grace as an excuse for acting disgracefully. Dr. Adrian Rogers, long-time pastor of the Bellevue Baptist Church in Memphis, TN, says that a believer should never live in such a way that he becomes a "disgrace to grace."

Not only should believers never abuse their liberty to their own detriment, but they should also never abuse it to the detriment of others. What may not spiritually damage a mature believer may be capable of doing a great deal of damage to a more spiritually immature believer. If a mature believer acts carelessly, his actions may disillusion the weaker believer or cause him to be tempted to such an extent that he is pulled back into sin. What believer would want that on his conscience?

But some object by asking, "Why should someone else's immaturity limit my personal freedom?" Paul answered this objection in his first letter to the believers at Corinth:

> "You say, 'I am allowed to do anything'—but not everything is helpful. You say, 'I am allowed to do anything'—but not everything is beneficial. Don't think only of your own good. Think of other Christians and what is best for them.
>
> Here's what you should do. You may eat any meat that is sold in the marketplace. Don't ask whether or not it was offered to idols, and then your conscience won't be bothered. For 'the earth is the Lord's, and everything in it.'
>
> If someone who isn't a Christian asks you home for dinner, go ahead; accept the invitation if you want to. Eat whatever is offered to you and don't ask any questions about it. Your conscience should not be bothered by this. But suppose someone warns you that this meat has been offered to an idol. Don't eat it, out of consideration for the conscience of the one who told you. It might not be a matter of conscience for you, but it is for the other person.

Now, why should my freedom be limited by what someone else thinks? If I can thank God for the food and enjoy it, why should I be condemned for eating it? Whatever you eat or drink or whatever you do, you must do all for the glory of God. Don't give offense to Jews or Gentiles or the church of God. That is the plan I follow, too. I try to please everyone in everything I do. I don't just do what I like or what is best for me, but what is best for them so they may be saved." 1 Corinthians 10:23–33, NLT

Here, Paul stresses that the weaker believer's welfare is of utmost importance. But many who drink insist that it "cramps their style" not to be able to drink. They often point to verses 29 and 30 of this passage to justify their drinking:

"Now, why should my freedom be limited by what someone else thinks? If I can thank God for the food and enjoy it, why should I be condemned for eating it?" 1 Corinthians 10:29–30, NLT

Since in this passage, Paul is primarily concerned with the welfare of the weaker believers, this is a very self-centered interpretation of these verses to say the least. I think it is significant that this passage never mentions alcohol specifically—but instead discusses Christians who were eating meat that had been offered as a sacrifice to an idol.

In Paul's day, after these meats were offered to idols, they were then often taken and sold at the market. Since mature believers understood that an idol was nothing but a hunk of wood or stone, they knew the meat was unaffected by the idol and was suitable for consumption. But those new believers who had recently been saved out of paganism, still immature in their understanding, believed that the meat was tainted by demons and was unfit for Christian consumption. So they were offended when mature believers ate these meats. Paul's advice to those who faced this dilemma was clear:

"Now let's talk about food that has been sacrificed to idols. You think that everyone should agree with your perfect knowledge. While knowledge may make us feel important, it is love that really builds up the church. Anyone who claims to know all the answers doesn't really know very much. But the person who loves God is the one God knows and cares for. So now, what about it? Should we eat meat that has been sacrificed to idols? Well, we all know that an idol is not really a god and that there is only one God and no other. According to some people, there are many so-called gods and many lords, both in heaven and on earth. But we know that there is only one God, the Father, who created everything, and we exist for him. And there is only one Lord, Jesus Christ, through whom God made everything and through whom we have been given life. However, not all Christians realize this. Some are accustomed to thinking of idols as being real, so when they eat food that has been offered to idols, they think of it as the worship of real gods, and their weak consciences are violated. It's true that we can't win God's approval by what we eat. We don't miss out on anything if we don't eat it, and we don't gain anything if we do. But you must be careful with this freedom of yours. Do not cause a brother or sister with a weaker conscience to stumble. You see, this is what can happen: weak Christians who think it is wrong to eat this food will see you eating in the temple of an idol. You know there's nothing wrong with it, but they will be encouraged to violate their conscience by eating food that has been dedicated to the idol. So because of your superior knowledge, a weak Christian, for whom Christ died, will be destroyed. And you are sinning against Christ when you sin against other Christians by encouraging them to do something they believe is wrong. If what I eat is going to make another Christian sin, I will never eat meat again as long as I live—for I don't want to make another Christian stumble." 1 Corinthians 8:1–13, NLT

For the sake of a weaker believer's conscience, Paul urged the more mature believers to restrain themselves by not fully exercising their freedom in Christ. The core of Paul's message was this: for the health of the whole body of Christ, the exercising of the believer's liberty should never cause another believer to stumble:

"Be careful, however, that the exercise of your freedom does not become a stumbling block to the weak." 1 Corinthians 8:9, NIV

Paul taught the believers at Rome the same thing:

"If your brother is distressed because of what you eat, you are no longer acting in love. Do not by your eating destroy your brother for whom Christ died . . . Do not destroy the work of God for the sake of food. All food is clean, but it is wrong for a man to eat anything that causes someone else to stumble. It is better not to eat meat or drink wine or to do anything else that will cause your brother to fall." Romans 14:15, 20–21, NIV

Note: Just because Paul mentions wine in this passage, we shouldn't jump to the conclusion that he was referring to fermented wine. Remember that it was not the regular practice of New Testament believers to consume intoxicating wines.

Just as many believers in the early church were offended and damaged spiritually when other believers ate meats offered to idols, today many believers (and unbelievers) are offended and damaged spiritually when believers drink alcohol. But to compare eating meat offered to an idol to drinking fermented wine is a mistake. Nowhere in Scripture were believers commanded not to eat meat offered to idols, but in numerous places (both in the Old and New Testaments) believers *were* warned about the dangerous effects of alcohol. Paul even went as far as to say that such a sin against a weaker believer is actually a sin against Christ:

> "When you sin against your brothers in this way and wound their weak conscience, you sin against Christ." 1 Corinthians 8:12, NIV

In his famous *A Commentary on the Whole Bible,* Matthew Henry wrote:

> "Those whom Christ hath redeemed with his most precious blood should be very precious and dear to us. If he had such compassion as to die for them, that they might not perish, we should have so much compassion for them as to deny ourselves, for their sakes, in various instances, and not use our liberty to their hurt, to occasion their stumbling, or hazard their ruin. That man has very little of the spirit of the Redeemer who had rather his brother should perish than himself be abridged, in any respect, of his liberty. He who hath the Spirit of Christ in him will love those whom Christ loved, so as to die for them, and will study to promote their spiritual and eternal warfare, and shun every thing that would unnecessarily grieve them, and much more every thing that would be likely to occasion their stumbling, or falling into sin . . . Injuries done to Christians are injuries to Christ, especially

to babes in Christ, to weak Christians; and most of all, involving them in guilt; wounding their consciences is wounding him."[173]

When speaking to believers about alcohol and drinking in the 1920s, Billy Sunday said:

> "Personal liberty is not personal license. I dare not exercise personal liberty if it infringes on the liberty of others . . . You have no right to vote for an institution [liquor industry] that is going to drag your sons and daughters to hell."[174]

This is why Paul wrote: "Whatever you eat or drink or whatever you do, you must do all for the glory of God," 1 Corinthians 10:31, NLT. Paul was not saying that a believer could drink alcohol to the glory of God, but was saying that everything a believer does, including eating and drinking, should be seen through the filter of God's glory and others' welfare. Whatever might mask His glory in the eyes of the unsaved, or might possibly discourage or frustrate a weaker believer should be stricken from the believer's can-do list. The crux of the matter is this: is drinking so important to someone that he is willing to spiritually harm another person to do it? Paul concludes the debate by saying:

> "If what I eat is going to make another Christian sin, I will never eat meat again as long as I live—for I don't want to make another Christian stumble." 1 Corinthians 8:13, NLT

When it comes to drinking, a believer should never drink one drop if it could cause someone to stumble—and it's clear that it does.

Chapter 12

S OMEONE IS WATCHING

I am convinced that deep down in their heart of hearts, all believers know that it is wrong for them to drink alcohol. They know that it damages their witness. They know that it discourages and confuses weaker believers. They know that it turns many unbelievers away from Christ. They know that no good thing ever comes from it. There's no doubt about it—they know it is w-r-o-n-g. The fact that most believers who drink normally try to hide it from others is proof of that.

In addition to the fact that drinking is wrong, believers don't need it. Take it from me; I've lived forty-five years without ever taking one drink and I haven't missed a thing. My life has been a full, exciting, and extremely rewarding one thus far and I haven't needed any help from alcohol. During my high school and college years, I had friends who drank. I watched as it dealt them nothing but misery. Since I didn't touch the stuff, I was able to avoid the pain and regret that it brought them. Numerous times, they even admitted to me that they wished that they didn't drink. In the years since, I have discovered that many of them actually respected me for not drinking.

Some may think that the reason I've never used alcohol is because I've lived a sheltered, easy life—but this simply is not true. My life has essentially been the same as everyone else's—I've had good times and bad times as well. But through it all, I can assure you that I've not been penalized one bit by staying away from alcohol. Just read the testimonies of the countless millions who have never had a drink or have kicked the habit of drinking and you'll discover thankful people who gladly testify of satisfying lives that have not been diminished in the least by the lack of liquor.

I think it is significant that the man Jesus called the greatest man who had ever lived, never had a drink of alcohol:

> "I assure you, of all who have ever lived, none is greater than John the Baptist." Matthew 11:11, NLT

Remember that since John the Baptist had taken a Nazirite vow, he did not drink wines of any type—fermented or unfermented (Luke 7:33). Do you think his abstinence had anything to do with Jesus' opinion of him? I can't say for sure, but I'm certain it didn't hurt.

If you drink, ask yourself this question: "What real good ever comes from it?" I've visited with many who drink or used to and none of them has ever been able to name one legitimately good thing that alcohol ever did for them. None have even been able to give me one spiritually good thing that alcohol could do for them. On the other hand, all have always been able to give me a long list of calamities it has caused in their lives. So I have to ask, "Why drink?"

When trying to decide whether or not to drink, John MacArthur suggests that a believer ask himself these questions:

1. Are the wines we drink today the same as those in the Bible?
2. Is drinking necessary?
3. Is drinking the best choice?
4. Is drinking destructive?
5. Can drinking become a destructive habit?
6. Is drinking offensive to other Christians?
7. Will drinking harm my Christian witness?
8. Am I really certain that it is not a sin to drink?[175]

In his message, "Be Not Drunk with Wine," he says:

> "The wine that was consumed then [Bible times] was not what we know necessarily as wine today. It was a concentrated grape juice with its fermentation and intoxicating property removed. The point I'm

making is this: You cannot defend wine drinking today on the basis that they drank wine then, unless you can prove that you're drinking the same thing they were drinking."[176]

J. A. Seiss, a Lutheran theologian who lived in the 1800s, wrote:

"The history of strong drink is the history of ruin, of tears, of blood. It is, perhaps, the greatest curse that has ever scourged the earth. It is one of depravity's worst fruits—a giant demon of destruction. Men talk of earthquakes, storms, floods, conflagrations, famine, pestilence, despotism, and war; but intemperance in the use of intoxicating drinks has sent a volume of misery and woe into the stream of this world's history, more fearful and terrific than either of them. It is the Amazon and Mississippi among the rivers of wretchedness. It is the Alexander and Napoleon among the warriors upon the peace and good of man. It is like the pale horse of the Apocalypse whose rider is Death, and at whose heels follow hell and destruction. It is an evil which is limited to no age, no continent, no nation, no party, no sex, no period of life. It has taken the poor man at his toil and the rich man at his desk, the senator in the halls of state and the drayman on the street, the young man in his festivities and the old man in his repose, the priest at the altar and the layman in the pew, and plunged them together into a common ruin. It has raged equally in times of war and in times of peace, in periods of depression and in periods of prosperity, in republics and in monarchies, among the civilized and among the savage. Since the time that Noah came out of the ark, and planted vineyards, and drank of their wines, we read in all the histories of its terrible doings, and never once lose sight of its black and bloody tracks."[177]

This brings us back to these critical questions:

- Is there a good reason why a believer should drink?
- Can alcohol possibly do enough good that it is worth risking the bad it can do?
- Is drinking worth damaging one's witness?
- Is it worth causing someone else to stumble spiritually?

Incredibly, a good number in the church today must think so, because in many Christian circles, drinking has become sinfully fashionable (64% of Protestants drink). It's anybody's guess what short and long term effects this will have on the church and its witness. In a world thoroughly confused over spiritual things, surely it cannot be positive.

I believe that the spiritual epidemic of drinking that is sweeping through the church only serves to further blur the already fuzzy line between the church and the world. Rather than heeding the Scriptural command:

> "For we are the temple of the living God. As God has said: 'I will live with them and walk among them, and I will be their God, and they will be my people.' Therefore come out from them and be separate, says the Lord. Touch no unclean thing, and I will receive you." 2 Corinthians 6:16–17, NIV

today's believers seem bent on discovering just how much like the world they can become and still call themselves Christians. All the while, they seem unmoved by the effect this has on the church and its witness. One thing is certain: the believer's position on alcohol will have a major impact on others—positive or negative.

A story from the life of a man known affectionately to me as Bro. Gilbert, the pastor of the church where I grew up, illustrates this fact perfectly:

When he was a teenager, Gilbert and a few of his buddies were out driving around in a pickup truck one Saturday night. Not much was going on that evening, so they decided to drive out to the countryside. They drove for a few miles to a familiar place, parked the truck, and piled out. As the driver got out, he pulled a bottle of whiskey from under the seat, took a drink, and passed it to one of the other guys. One by one, each took a drink, and then passed it on around the circle. As the bottle made its way toward him, Gilbert was faced with a huge dilemma: either take a drink and run the risk of ruining his witness (all of the guys knew he was a Christian) or pass the bottle by and run the risk of facing ridicule from his friends or worse yet, being black-balled by the group.

As he fought the battle in his mind, the bottle, slowly, but surely made its way toward him. Gilbert wondered, *What should I do?* When the young man next to him finished his drink, he handed Gilbert the bottle and all eyes immediately turned to him. As he held the bottle in his hand, Gilbert made his decision, took the risk, and passed the bottle on without taking a drink. The guys all had a good laugh, but nothing much more came of it. After a few more drinks, they all climbed back into the truck and drove home.

To his surprise, in the days that followed, none of the guys said anything about the "drinking incident." Instead, everyone went about as if nothing had ever happened. Gilbert remained in the group's good graces, his witness remained intact, and all was well with the world. Time passed, as it always does, and his Saturday night battle with the bottle quickly faded into the past—or so he thought. One by one, the guys all left home, got married, started careers and gradually lost touch with one another.

Years later, Gilbert was walking down the sidewalk when a man approached him and began to strike up a conversation. He turned out to be one of the guys from the group whom Gilbert hadn't seen in years. As they caught up on each other, he finally asked Gilbert, "Do you remember the night all of us went out in the country to have a drink?" Gilbert responded, "I sure do, but it's been years since I've thought about that. What makes you ask?" The man said, "Gilbert, you may not have known it then, but I had been studying your life for quite some time. I knew you were a Christian and I was watching you to see if Christianity was real. That night as we passed the bottle around, I waited anxiously to see what you would do. When you passed the bottle by and didn't take a drink, it made a big impression on me. Although you may have worried that we would look down on you for not drinking, we didn't. Your courage to stand up for your convictions, even when it could have cost you our friendship, made a big impact on all of us. I never forgot what you did. In fact, your stand played a big role in my coming to Christ. I'm a Christian today because you didn't take a drink that night. Because you passed the bottle by, I'm going to go to heaven someday. Thank you for saying 'no' to alcohol."

If someone is watching you like those guys watched Gilbert, will they think more or less of Christ and Christianity because of what you do? Someday in eternity, will someone walk up to you and say, "I'm going to heaven because you didn't drink"? Or will someone say, "Because you just had to have a drink, I decided Christianity was just a joke and now I'm going to spend eternity in Hell"? Be assured of this: if you claim to be a Christian, someone is watching.

I don't know about you, but that not only shakes me, it stirs me down to my core. I hope it shakes and stirs you as well. Before you take that next drink, think about the person who may be watching and then ask yourself, "Is it worth it?"

Footnotes

[1] *Bible Wines or Laws of Fermentation and Wines of the Ancients,* Rev William Patton, 1871, title page, pp.11–12.

[2] *The Oklahoman,* Saturday, Sept. 18, 2004, page 1A, 3A.

[3] National Research Council Institute of Medicine, "Reducing Underage Drinking: A Collective Responsibility." 2004, Agricultural Marketing Service, 2002. MADD website.

[4] Strasburger, V. C. & Donnerstein, E. (1999). Children, adolescents, and the media: Issues and solutions. American Academy of Pediatrics, 103, 1–15.

[5] Special Report, "Fewer Drops in the Bucket: Alcohol Industry 'Responsibility' Declined on TV in 2002." The Center on Alcohol Marketing & Youth.

[6] American Academy of Pediatrics: "Alcohol Use and Abuse: A Pediatric Concern," *Pediatrics,* Vol. 108, No. 1, July 2001, pp. 185–189.

[7] Sheldon Gottlieb, MD, *Diabetes Forecast,* Apr. 2004, TheraSense website, "Ask the Educator."

[8] Walter B. Knight, *Knight's Up-to-the-Minute Illustrations* (Chicago: Moody Press, 1974), p.70, Dr. Jack Van Impe & Roger F. Campbell, *Alcohol: The Beloved Enemy* (Thomas Nelson Publisher, Nashville, TN, 1980), p.47.

[9] 10th Special Report to the US Congress on Alcohol and Health. National Institute on Alcohol Abuse and Alcoholism: Washington, DC, 2000.

[10] "Whiskey Lullaby", by Bill Anderson and Jon Randall, ©2003 EMI April Music, Inc./Sea Gayle Music (ASCAP).

[11] National Association of Convenience Stores, "That's the Spirit–U.S. Alcohol Sales Growing," Mar. 6, 2003.

[12] National Association of Convenience Stores, "That's the Spirit–U.S. Alcohol Sales Growing," Mar. 6, 2003.

[13] The University of Minnesota, *Self-Protection Series: Alcohol Decisions,* "Alcohol Abuse is a Serious Problem," by Sharon K.B. Wright, copyright 2002.

[14] *Primer* 3, "A Sound Investment: Identifying and Treating Alcohol Problems," Henrick Harwood, Expert Consultant. Jeffrey Hon., April 2003, The George Washington University Medical Center

[15] U.S. Census Bureau, "State Government Tax Collections: 2001," revised April 2003.

[16] The Beer Institute, "New Report Details Beer Industry's Significant Contributions to the American Economy," April 15, 2003.

[17] National Institute on Alcohol Abuse and Alcoholism, News Releases, "Surgeon General Calls on Americans to Face Facts About Drinking," April 1, 2004.

[18] MSNBC News, "Alcohol linked to 75,000 U.S. deaths a year," Sept. 24, 2004, www.msnbc.msn.com.

[19] "Why has MADD changed its mission statement?" Mothers Against Drunk Driving website, 2005.

[20] About Suicide, "Facts About Suicide," www.afsp.org, The National Center for Health Statistics, 2001.

[21] *Current Health 2,* "Suicide: what causes someone to commit suicide–and what can you do about it?" by Nina M. Riccio, copyright 2004, Weekly Reader Corp.

[22] *Self-Protection Series: Alcohol Decisions,* "Alcohol Abuse is a Serious Problem," by Sharon K.B. Wright, University of Minnesota Extension Service, copyright 2002 Regents of the University of Minnesota.

[23] The Community Health Improvement Partners, "2001 Community Health Needs Assessment," San Diego, CA, www.sdchip.org.

[24] MSNBC News, "Alcohol linked to 75,000 U.S. deaths a year," Sept. 24, 2004, www.msnbc.msn.com.

[25] The U.S. Department of Health and Human Services, "Alcohol: What You Don't Know Can Harm You," U.S. Dept. of Health & Human Services website.

[26] "Deaths: Final Data for 2001," NCHS, CDC, "Statistics about Cirrhosis of the liver," WrongDiagnosis.com.

[27] "Report: Alcohol abuse up, but fewer alcoholics," Fri., June 11, 2004, WASHINGTON (Reuters), CNN.com.

[28] Ninth Special Report on the U.S. Congress on Alcohol & Health. U.S. Dept. of Health & Human Services, NIAAA, June 1997, Frederick Stinson, Samar DeBakey, Bridget Grant & Deborah Dawson, "Association of alcohol problems with risk for AIDS in the 1988 National Health Interview Study." Alcohol Health and Research World, NIAAA, 16(3): 245–252, 1992, "Millennium Hangover: Keeping Score on Alcohol." Drug Strategies.

[29] S. A. Smith-Warner, D. Spiegelman, S.S. Yaun, "Alcohol & breast cancer in women: A pooled analysis of cohort studies." Journal of the American Medical Assoc., 279(7): 535–540, 1998, "Millennium Hangover: Keeping Score on Alcohol." Drug Strategies.

[30] The National Center for Chronic Disease Prevention and Health Promotion, *Alcohol and Public Health,* "General Alcohol Information: Measures of Alcohol Consumption and Alcohol-related Health Effects from Excessive Consumption," August 4, 2004, www.cdc.gov.

[31] Billy Sunday, "The Trail of the Serpent," 1917 sermon, *The Sword of the Lord,* July 14, 1967, *Alcohol: The Beloved Enemy,* by Dr. Jack Van Impe, with Roger F. Campbell, Thomas Nelson Publisher, 1980, p.39.

[32] "Traffic Safety Facts 2003–Alcohol." U.S. Dept. of Transportation, National Highway Traffic Safety Administration, National Center for Statistics & Analysis.

[33] "Traffic Safety Facts 2003–Alcohol." U.S. Dept. of Transportation, National Highway Traffic Safety Administration, National Center for Statistics & Analysis.

[34] "2001 National Survey on Drinking & Driving," Gallup Organization, 2003, MADD website, General Statistics.

[35] National Highway Traffic Safety Administration, 2001, MADD website, General Statistics.

[36] National Highway Traffic Safety Administration, 2003, MADD website, General Statistics.

[37] NHTSA, "Traffic Safety Facts 2003–Alcohol".

[38] MADD website, General Statistics, Runge, Jeffrey W. M.D. Administrator, DOT, MADD Impaired Driving Summit, Jan. 2002.

[39] "Traffic Safety Facts 2003–Alcohol." U.S. Dept. of Transportation, National Highway Traffic Safety Administration, National Center for Statistics & Analysis.

[40] Ninth Special Report to the U.S. Congress on Alcohol & Health. U.S. Dept. of Health & Human Services, National Institute on Alcohol Abuse & Alcoholism, June 1997.

[41] "Age of drinking onset & involvement in physical fights after drinking." Hingson R., Heeren T., Zakocs R., Dept. of Social & Behavioral Sciences, Boston University of Public Health, Boston, MA, 2001.

[42] The National Center for Chronic Disease Prevention and Health Promotion, *Alcohol and Public Health: General Alcohol Information,* "Measures of Alcohol Consumption and Alcohol-related Health Effects from Excessive Consumption," CDC website, www.cdc.gov, August 4, 2004.

[43] *Self-Protection Series: Alcohol Decisions,* "Alcohol Abuse is a Serious Problem," by Sharon K.B. Wright, University of Minnesota Extension Service, copyright 2002, Regents of the University of Minnesota.

[44] Alcohol Awareness Fact Sheet, Bellarmine University, Louisville, Kentucky, 2005 website, www.1.bellarmine.edu.

[45] The U.S. Department of Health and Human Services, "Youth and Underage Drinking: An Overview," 2004 website.

[46] The U.S. Department of Health and Human Services, Sept. 4, 2002, The American Medical Association, "Reducing

Underage Drinking. A Collective Responsibility–fact sheet on the 2003 Institute of Medicine study," December 4, 2004, www.ama-assn.org.

[47] "Summary of Findings from the 2002 National Survey on Drug Use and Health," U.S. Department of Health and Human Services, 2003.

[48] "Pediatricians Call For Ban On All Alcohol Advertising In The Media." American Academy of Pediatrics, Washington Office, Dec. 20, 2001.

[49] Strasburger, V. C. & Donnerstein, E. (1999). Children, adolescents, and the media: Issues and solutions. American Academy of Pediatrics, 103, 1–15.

[50] "Teen Tipplers: America's Underage Drinking Epidemic," The National Center on Addiction and Substance Abuse at Columbia University, 633 Third Avenue, New York, NY, 10017–6706, revised February 2003.

[51] *Monitoring the Future,* The University of Michigan, Ann Arbor, Michigan, Lloyd Johnson, et al., December 21, 2004.

[52] Institute of Medicine, "Reducing Underage Drinking: A Collective Responsibility," September 2003.

[53] The U.S. Department of Health and Human Services, "Youth and Underage Drinking: An Overview," 2004 website.

[54] Drug Strategies, "Millennium Hangover: Keeping Score on Alcohol," 1999.

[55] "Alcohol Use and Abuse: A Pediatric Concern," *Pediatrics*, Vol. 108, No. 1, July 2001, pp. 185–189, The American Academy of Pediatrics.

[56] *Journal of Studies on Alcohol,* "College Drinking, What It Is, and What To Do about It: A Review of the State of Science," Mark S. Goldman, PhD., Associate Director of the NIAAA, p.5, NIAAA Reports. March 2002.

[57] Henry Wechsler, "Changes in Binge Drinking and Related Problems Among American College Students Between 1993 & 1997: Results of the Harvard School of Public Health

College Alcohol Study." Journal of American College Health. 47:57–68, 1998.

[58] Henry Wechsler, "Changes in Binge Drinking and Related Problems Among American College Students Between 1993 & 1997: Results of the Harvard School of Public Health College Alcohol Study." Journal of American College Health. 47:57–68, 1998.

[59] *Journal of Studies on Alcohol,* "College Drinking, What It Is, and What To Do about It: A Review of the State of Science," Mark S. Goldman, PhD., Associate Director of the NIAAA, p.5, NIAAA Reports. March 2002.

[60] Drug Strategies, "Millennium Hangover: Keeping Score on Alcohol," 1999.

[61] *The Oklahoman,* Sunday, November 7, 2004, 10A.

[62] *The Oklahoman,* Sunday, November 7, 2004, 1A, 10A.

[63] Online News Hour, The News Hour Health Unit, "Binge Drinking." Apr. 10, 2002.

[64] Henry Wechsler, "Changes in Binge Drinking and Related Problems Among American College Students Between 1993 & 1997: Results of the Harvard School of Public Health College Alcohol Study." Journal of American College Health. 47:57–68, 1998.

[65] Henry Wechsler, "Binge Drinking, Tobacco and Illicit Drug Use and Involvement in College Athletics: A Survey of Students at 140 American Colleges." Journal of American College Health. 45:195–200, 1997

[66] *The Oklahoman,* Sunday, November 7, 2004, 10A.

[67] *Whiskey For My Men and Beer For My Horses,* (© Tokeco Tunes/Sony-ATV Songs LLC dba Tree Publishing Co./Big Yellow Dog Music.).

[68] "Tragic Consequences of Alcohol Dependence Underscore Need for Screening, Education," *Psychiatric News,* Vol. 36, N0.3, February 2, 2001, p. 6.

[69] The National Center for Chronic Disease Prevention and Health Promotion, "Measures of Alcohol Consumption and

Alcohol-Related Health Effects from Excessive Consumption," August 4, 2004.

[70] Thomas W. Mangione, Jonathan Howland and Marianne Lee, "New Perspectives for Worksite Alcohol Strategies: Results from a Corporate Drinking Study." Funded by Robert Wood Johnson Foundation and National Institute on Alcohol Abuse and Alcoholism, Dec. 1998.

[71] "Alcoholism, An Agonized Plea For Love," by Farrell and Wilbur Cross, *Cosmopolitan*, July 1961.

[72] "The Treatment of Drinking Problems: A guide for the helping professions." Griffith Edwards, E. Jane Marshall, Christopher C.H. Cook, Cambridge University Press, 2003.

[73] "Booze" by Billy Sunday, www.believers.com

[74] *Alcohol: The Beloved Enemy*, by Dr. Jack Van Impe, with Roger F. Campbell, Thomas Nelson Publisher, 1980, p. 70–71, Walter B. Knight, *Knight's Treasury of Illustrations* (Grand Rapids: Wm. B. Eerdmans Pub. Co., 1963), p. 400.

[75] "Q&A: Alcohol General." March 2004, Insurance Institute for Highway Safety website.

[76] "Q&A: Alcohol General." March 2004, Insurance Institute for Highway Safety website.

[77] "Alcohol: How Much is Too Much?" National Highway Traffic Safety Administration, 2002, MADD Online, Alcohol Stats & Resources.

[78] "Alcohol: How Much is Too Much?" National Highway Traffic Safety Administration, 2002, MADD Online, Alcohol Stats & Resources.

[79] "Q&A: Alcohol General." March 2004, Insurance Institute for Highway Safety website.

[80] "Q&A: Alcohol General." March 2004, Insurance Institute for Highway Safety website. Zador, P.L.; Krawchuk, S. A.; and Voas, R.B. 2000. Alcohol-related relative risk of driver fatalities and driver involvement in fatal crashes in relation to driver age and gender: an update using 1996 data. *Journal of Studies on Alcohol* 61(3): 387–395.

[81] "Biological Impacts of Alcohol Use: An Overview." Michaele P. Dunlap, Psy.D, MADD website, "Stats & Resources: The Brain".

[82] "Biological Impacts of Alcohol Use: An Overview." Michaele P. Dunlap, Psy.D, MADD website, "Stats & Resources: The Brain".

[83] "Biological Impacts of Alcohol Use: An Overview." By Michaele P. Dunlap, Psy.D, www.oregoncounseling.org.

[84] "Moderate alcohol use may be associated with brain shrinkage." Dec. 2003, American Heart Association, www.science-blog.com, Jingzhong Ding, Ph.D., Bloomberg School of Public Health, Johns Hopkins University, Baltimore, MD.

[85] Moderate alcohol use may be associated with brain shrinkage." Dec. 2003, American Heart Association, www.sciencblog.com.

[86] White, 2001, MADD website, "Stats & Resources: The Brain".

[87] "Biological Impacts Of Alcohol Use: An Overview." By Michaele P. Dunlap, Psy.D,
www.oregoncounseling.org.

[88] "Biological Impacts Of Alcohol Use: An Overview." By Michaele P. Dunlap, Psy.D, www.oregoncounseling.org.

[89] "Alcohol Awareness: The effect on the body," June 2002, Alcohol Awareness week in association with BBC Radio Nottingham (95.5 & 103.8FM): "The Breakfast Show" with Karl Cooper, "The Mid Morning Show" with Jeff Owen, and "The Afternoon Show" with Brian Tansley.

[90] K.M. Dubowski, Intoximeters Incorporated website, www.intox.com

[91] "Basic Alcohol Information," Michigan State University, 2002, justthefacts.msu.edu.

[92] "Basic Alcohol Information," Michigan State University, 2002, justthefacts.msu.edu.

[93] J.A. Seiss, *The Gospel in Leviticus* (Grand Rapids: Zondervan, n.d.), p. 183, *Alcohol: The Beloved Enemy*, by Dr. Jack Van

Impe, with Roger F. Campbell, Thomas Nelson Publisher, 1980, p. 134.

[94] "Alcohol," Health Opponents, www.mcvitamins.com.

[95] "Alcohol," Health Opponents, www.mcvitamins.com.

[96] "Biological Impacts of Alcohol Use: An Overview." By Michaele P. Dunlap, Psy.D, www.oregoncounseling.org.

[97] Deaths: Final Data for 2001, National Center for Health Statistics, Center for Disease Control.

[98] Drug Strategies, "Millennium Hangover: Keeping Score on Alcohol," 1999, www.drugstrategies.org.

[99] Drinksense Factsheets: "Alcohol–the effects on the body." www.gurney.co.uk/drinksense/factsheets, "Biological Impacts Of Alcohol Use: An Overview." By Michaele P. Dunlap, Psy.D, www. oregoncounseling.org.

[100] "We Need Prohibition," *The Baptist Pillar*, published by Bible Baptist Church, Brandon, MB R7A 3J7, John Reaves, Sr., editor & pastor, baptistpillar.com.

[101] Laertius Diogenes, *Lives & Opinions of Eminent Philosophers*, Pythagoras (VI), worldofquotes.com.

[102] Lucius Annaeus Seneca, Epistoloe Ad Lucilium LXXXIII, worldofquotes.com.

[103] *The Spirits of Our Forefathers*, by Thomas Jewett.

[104] *A Brief History of Social Reform, The Temperance Movement and Prohibition in the United States*, by Lee McKenzie.

[105] www.prohibitionists.org/QQ-alcohol.htm.

[106] "Temperance Address." Abraham Lincoln Online, www.showcase.netins.net, *Collected Works of Abraham Lincoln*, edited by Roy P. Basler.

[107] *Alcohol: The Beloved Enemy*, by Jack Van Impe, with Roger F. Campbell, Thomas Nelson Publishers, Nashville, TN, 1980, p. 81–82, Walter B. Knight, *Knight's Master Book of New Illustrations* (Grand Rapids: Wm. B. Eerdmans Pub. Co., 1956), p. 671.

[108] "Booze" by Billy Sunday, www.biblebelievers.com.

[109] Sir Arnold Toynbee, *Civilizations on Trial: Essays*, New York: Oxford University Press, 1948.

[110] Bertrand Russell, *The Conquest of Happiness*, London: George Allen and Unwin; New York: Horace Liveright, 1930.

[111] "Alcohol Abuse," Psychological Assessment Referral & Treatment Services, Austin, TX, www.psycharts.com/alcohol.htm.

[112] www.prohibitionists.org/QQ-alcohol.htm.

[113] www.prohibitionists.org/QQ-alcohol.htm.

[114] John MacArthur, *Living in the Spirit* message series, "Be Not Drunk with Wine," book of Ephesians 5:18, Part 3.

[115] *Bible Wines or Laws of Fermentation & Wines of the Ancients*, by Rev. William Patton, D.D., 1871, pp. 27–113.

[116] *Bible Wines or Laws of Fermentation & Wines of the Ancients*, by Rev. William Patton, D.D., 1871, p.63.

[117] John Stuart Mill, *System of Logic, Bible Wines or Laws of Fermentation & Wines of the Ancients*, by Rev. William Patton, D.D., 1871, pp. 63–64.

[118] *Bible Wines or Laws of Fermentation & Wines of the Ancients*, by Rev. William Patton, D.D., 1871, pp. 33 & 57.

[119] *Living in the Spirit*, "Be Not Drunk with Wine–Part 2", message by John MacArthur.

[120] *Bible Wines or Laws of Fermentation & Wines of the Ancients*, by Rev. William Patton, D.D., 1871, p. 53, Professor Moses Stuart, *Letter to Dr. Nott*, 1848.

[121] *Bible Wines or Laws of Fermentation & Wines of the Ancients*, by Rev. William Patton, D.D., 1871, p 32, Rev. Henry Homes, *Bibliotheca Sacra*, May 1848.

[122] Rev. William Patton, D.D., *Bible Wines or Laws of Fermentation & Wines of the Ancients*, 1871, pp.16–17.

[123] Rev. William Patton, D.D., *Bible Wines or Laws of Fermentation & Wines of the Ancients*, 1871, p.17.

[124] Charles Wesley Ewing, *The Bible and Its Wines, published by Denver: Prohibition National Committee, 1949, p. 17,*

[125] John MacDougall, "The Fungus among Us: A Primer on Yeast," April 1998

126 *Bible Wines or Laws of Fermentation & Wines of the Ancients*, by Rev. William Patton, D.D., 1871, p 33, Rev. Dr. Jacobus

127 *Bible Wines or Laws of Fermentation & Wines of the Ancients*, by Rev. William Patton, D.D., 1871, pp. 24–25

128 *Living in the Spirit*, "Be Not Drunk with Wine–Part 2," by John MacArthur

129 *Bible Wines or Laws of Fermentation & Wines of the Ancients*, by Rev. William Patton, D.D., 1871,

130 *Living in the Spirit*, "Be Not Drunk with Wine–Part 2," by John MacArthur, and *Bible Wines or Laws of Fermentation & Wines of the Ancients*, by Rev. William Patton, D.D., 1871, pp. 55–64.

131 *Bible Wines or Laws of Fermentation & Wines of the Ancients*, by Rev. William Patton, D.D., 1871, p. 74.

132 Ed Rickard, Ph.D., *What the Bible Teaches about Alcoholic Drink*, "Lesson 2: Texts in Praise of Wine," Bible Studies at the Moorings, www.themoorings.org.

133 *Alcohol: The Beloved Enemy*, by Jack Van Impe, with Roger F. Campbell, Thomas Nelson Publishers, Nashville, TN, 1980, pp. 87–100.

134 "Economic Strategies for Prevention," speech by William Plymat, executive director, American Council on Alcohol Problems, *Alcohol: The Beloved Enemy*, by Jack Van Impe, with Roger F. Campbell, Thomas Nelson Publishers, Nashville, TN, 1980, pp. 160–161.

135 Ed Rickard, Ph.D., *What the Bible Teaches about Alcoholic Drink*, "Lesson 1: The Case for Abstinence," Bible Studies at the Moorings, www.themoorings.org.

136 Dr. John J. Owen, *Commentary, Bible Wines or Laws of Fermentation & Wines of the Ancients*, by Rev. William Patton, D.D., 1871, pp. 81–82.

137 Gene Griessman, *The Words Lincoln Lived By: 52 Timeless Principles To Light Your Path*, pub. by Fireside/Simon & Schuster, www.presidentlincoln.com

[138] *Bible Wines or Laws of Fermentation & Wines of the Ancients*, by Rev. William Patton, D.D., 1871, p. 89.

[139] Dr. S. M. Isaacs, *Bible Wines or Laws of Fermentation & Wines of the Ancients*, by Rev. William Patton, D.D., 1871, pp. 83–84.

[140] *Bible Wines or Laws of Fermentation & Wines of the Ancients*, by Rev. William Patton, D.D., 1871, p. 90.

[141] *Bible Wines or Laws of Fermentation & Wines of the Ancients*, by Rev. William Patton, D.D., 1871, p. 91.

[142] *Bible Wines or Laws of Fermentation & Wines of the Ancients*, by Rev. William Patton, D.D., 1871, p. 91.

[143] *Bible Wines or Laws of Fermentation & Wines of the Ancients*, by Rev. William Patton, D.D., 1871, p. 92.

[144] *Bible Wines or Laws of Fermentation & Wines of the Ancients*, by Rev. William Patton, D.D., 1871, p. 92.

[145] John R. Rice, *The Son of God*, p. 50, Sword of the Lord Publishers, 1976.

[146] *Bible Wines or Laws of Fermentation & Wines of the Ancients*, by Rev. William Patton, D.D., 1871, p. 90.

[147] R.A. Torrey, *Difficulties in the Bible, Alcohol: The Beloved Enemy*, by Jack Van Impe, with Roger F. Campbell, Thomas Nelson Publishers, Nashville, TN, 1980, p. 125.

[148] William L. Pettingill, *Bible Questions Answered*, pp. 223–224, *Alcohol: The Beloved Enemy*, by Jack Van Impe, with Roger F. Campbell, Thomas Nelson Publishers, Nashville, TN, 1980, p. 125.

[149] Gerald L. Borchert, Ph.D., *The New American Commentary: An Exegetical and Theological Exposition of Holy Scripture, John 12–21*, pp. 152–153, Broadman & Holman Publishers, 1996.

[150] *Bible Wines or Laws of Fermentation & Wines of the Ancients*, by Rev. William Patton, D.D., 1871, p. 79.

[151] *Bible Wines or Laws of Fermentation & Wines of the Ancients*, by Rev. William Patton, D.D., 1871, p. 79–80.

[152] *Bible Wines or Laws of Fermentation & Wines of the Ancients*, by Rev. William Patton, D.D., 1871, p. 79.

153 John MacArthur, Jr., *The MacArthur New Testament Commentary: Matthew 8–15*, The Moody Bible Institute, Chicago, publisher, 1987, pp. 69–70

154 *Bible Wines or Laws of Fermentation & Wines of the Ancients*, by Rev. William Patton, D.D., 1871, p. 83.

155 *Bible Wines or Laws of Fermentation & Wines of the Ancients*, by Rev. William Patton, D.D., 1871, p. 83.

156 *Thayer*, p. 71, *Bible Wines or Laws of Fermentation & Wines of the Ancients*, by Rev. William Patton, D.D., 1871, p. 84.

157 Rev. A. P. Peabody, D.D., *Monthly Review*, Jan. 1870, p. 41, *Bible Wines or Laws of Fermentation & Wines of the Ancients*, by Rev. William Patton, D.D., 1871, p. 84.

158 *Bible Wines or Laws of Fermentation & Wines of the Ancients*, by Rev. William Patton, D.D., 1871, p. 84–87.

159 Dr. W. A. Criswell, *Great Doctrines of the Bible, Vol. 3: Ecclesiology*, Zondervan Publishing House: Grand Rapids, MI, 1983, p. 81.

160 *Bible Wines or Laws of Fermentation & Wines of the Ancients*, by Rev. William Patton, D.D., 1871, p. 87.

161 *Bible Wines or Laws of Fermentation & Wines of the Ancients*, by Rev. William Patton, D.D., 1871, pp. 111–112.

162 John MacArthur, Jr., *The MacArthur New Testament Commentary: 1 Timothy*, The Moody Bible Institute, Chicago, publisher, 1995, pp. 151–153.

163 William Barclay, *The Letters to Timothy, Titus, and Philemon* , Philadelphia: Westminster, publishers, 1975, 93–94, John MacArthur, Jr., *The MacArthur New Testament Commentary: 1 Timothy*, The Moody Bible Institute, Chicago, publisher, 1995, pp. 152–153.

164 Ed Rickard, Ph.D., *What the Bible Teaches about Alcoholic Drink*, "Lesson 3: Other Texts Cited by Moderationists," Bible Studies at the Moorings, www.themoorings.org.

165 "Alcohol, Wine, and Cardiovascular Disease," the American Heart Association, Dec. 16, 2004.

166 "Red Wine–Heart Health Benefits?" by Gloria Tsang, R.D., Healthcastle.com.

167 "Nutrition Advisor," Yale-New Haven Hospital, New Haven, CT., ynhh.org/online/nutrition /advisor/red_wine.html.

168 Charles Wesley Ewing, *The Bible and Its Wines* (Denver: Prohibition National Committee, 1949), p. 22, *Alcohol: The Beloved Enemy*, by Jack Van Impe, with Roger F. Campbell, Thomas Nelson Publishers, Nashville, TN, 1980, p. 138.

169 *Alcohol: The Beloved Enemy*, by Jack Van Impe, with Roger F. Campbell, Thomas Nelson Publishers, Nashville, TN, 1980, p. 137.

170 Ed Rickard, Ph.D., *What the Bible Teaches about Alcoholic Drink*, "Lesson 1: The Case for Abstinence," Bible Studies at the Moorings, www.themoorings.org.

171 John MacArthur, *Living in the Spirit* message series, "Be Not Drunk with Wine, part 2".

172 John R. W. Stott, *The Message of Romans*, "God's good news for the world," Inter-Varsity Press, Leicester, England, Drover's Grove, Illinois, USA, 1994, pp. 58–60.

173 Matthew Henry, *A Commentary on the Whole Bible*, 1 Corinthians 8, p. 547.

174 "Booze" by Billy Sunday, www.biblebelievers.com.

175 John MacArthur, "Be Not Drunk with Wine," *The Spirit-filled Life: Ephesians*, message series.

176 *Living in the Spirit*, "Be Not Drunk with Wine–Part 2, by John MacArthur.

177 Joseph A. Seiss, *The Gospel in Leviticus* (Grand Rapids: Zondervan, n.d.), pp. 180–181, *Alcohol: The Beloved Enemy*, by Jack Van Impe, with Roger F. Campbell, Thomas Nelson Publishers, Nashville, TN, 1980, pp. 104–105.

Visit the Trinity Baptist Church in Yukon, OK at
www.trinityyukon.com

Contact author Dan Fisher
or order more copies of this book at

TATE PUBLISHING, LLC

127 East Trade Center Terrace
Mustang, Oklahoma 73064

(888) 361 - 9473

Tate Publishing, LLC

www.tatepublishing.com